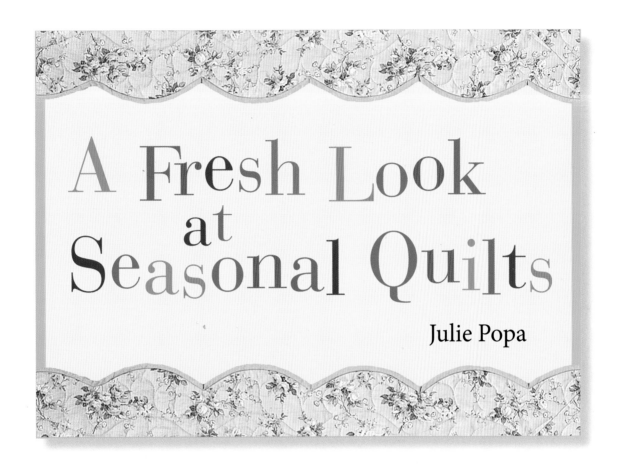

A Fresh Look
at
Seasonal Quilts

Julie Popa

Martingale®
& COMPANY

Dedication

To my husband, Sean, and my children, Shanae, Alexis, Jaclyn, and Stockton, who have eaten more than their share of cereal for dinner during this book's creation.

Acknowledgments

My thanks to:

Sean, Shanae, Alexis, Jaclyn, and Stockton for your patience, love, and support throughout this labor of love. I couldn't have done it without you.

Paula Murray for taking good designs and turning them into beautiful quilts so quickly.

Yvonne Fonnesbeck; I love you, Mom! Thank you for the long hours of hand stitching that helped me accomplish this.

Paul Fonnesbeck for caring so much about my well-being and always looking out for his little girl.

Bette Popa for all of the help, babysitting, support, and encouragement that you provided.

Alean Popa for watching the kids and sharing in my excitement.

Blake Fonnesbeck for your encouragement in my quest to make quilts for my friends and family!

The staff at Martingale & Company for your patience as I learned the process of creating a book and for seeing my vision and putting it to print.

A Fresh Look at Seasonal Quilts
© 2006 by Julie Popa

That Patchwork Place® is an imprint of Martingale & Company®.

Martingale & Company
20205 144th Avenue NE
Woodinville, WA 98072-8478 USA
www.martingale-pub.com

Credits

President: Nancy J. Martin
CEO: Daniel J. Martin
COO: Tom Wierzbicki
Publisher: Jane Hamada
Editorial Director: Mary V. Green
Managing Editor: Tina Cook
Technical Editor: Cyndi Hershey
Copy Editor: Melissa Bryan
Design Director: Stan Green
Illustrator: Laurel Strand
Cover Designer: Stan Green
Text Designer: Trina Craig
Photographer: Brent Kane

Printed in China
11 10 09 08 07 06   8 7 6 5 4 3 2 1

Library of Congress Cataloging-in-Publication Data
Library of Congress Control Number: 2006008579

ISBN-13: 978-1-56477-680-8
ISNB-10: 1-56477-680-8

MISSION STATEMENT

Dedicated to providing quality products and service to inspire creativity.

Contents

Introduction ◆ 4

Working with Wool ◆ 5

Quiltmaking Tips ◆ 9

Winter

Snowflake Lap Quilt ◆ 14

Warm Hearts Table Topper ◆ 18

Be My Valentine Wall Hanging ◆ 24

Heartfelt Wool Table Runner ◆ 30

Spring

Spring Is Sprung Quilt ◆ 32

Spring Penny Rug ◆ 41

Iris Wool Table Runner ◆ 44

Spring Bouquet Table Topper ◆ 49

Sunshine Lap Quilt ◆ 55

Summer

Summertime Picnic Quilt ◆ 57

Cherries Wool Table Runner ◆ 60

Fruit Salad Wall Hanging ◆ 63

Star-Spangled Lap Quilt ◆ 68

America the Beautiful Table Topper ◆ 71

Fall

Autumn Splendor Wall Hanging ◆ 76

Autumn Leaves Penny Rug ◆ 79

Fall Harvest Table Topper ◆ 82

Pumpkin Patch Lap Quilt ◆ 88

Pumpkin Wool Table Runner ◆ 92

About the Author ◆ 96

Introduction

This book features a variety of fun seasonal projects for quilters of all skill levels. I love to combine piecing and appliqué, and each season provides perfect inspiration for this. Using my interior design background, I've created colorful projects that can be used to decorate your home throughout the year or give to a friend. This book includes appliquéd wool projects and projects that combine wool with cotton piecing. Embroidery accents have been added to both types. Quilters can piece a quilt on the weekend or create a convenient embroidery travel project. May these quilts bring enjoyment to you each new season.

Working with Wool

Wool and wool felt add a new texture and dimension when incorporated into a quilt or other project. That is why I chose to use them in so many of the projects in this book. Of course, any of the appliqué designs shown with wool can easily be made using cotton fabrics and your preferred method of appliqué. The results will be just as beautiful. In creating so many projects with wool, I have developed some techniques that work quite well.

True 100% wool is rich in color. It also dyes better than wool blends, so custom colors can be created beautifully. It is the most expensive of the wool products, but most projects include only one or two larger pieces, with small pieces for the appliqué. This wool has a tendency to fray easily. It is sold by the yard on 54"-wide bolts or as smaller cut pieces.

Wool blends contain up to 70% wool; the balance usually consists of nylon. Like 100% wool, blends are sold by the yard on 54"-wide bolts or as smaller cut pieces. Wool felt contains 20% to 35% wool, with rayon making up the balance. This wool is sold on either 36"- or 72"-wide bolts as well as in smaller pieces. Both wool blends and wool felt have some advantages over 100% wool. They are less expensive, while still available in many colors. Wool blends don't fray easily, and wool felt doesn't fray at all, so I recommend these fabrics for any narrow appliqué pieces such as vines or stems.

I enjoy mixing various types of wool within the same project. In this book, if you see wool listed in a materials list, it refers to either 100% wool or a wool blend. For "Iris Wool Table Runner," shown on page 44, I wanted a backing fabric that could hold scalloped edging without fraying, even if I didn't add finishing stitches. For that project I specifically chose wool felt for the backing, as noted in the materials list.

UNDERSTANDING WOOL

Wool doesn't have a right side or a wrong side. It's dyed, and any patterns in the fabric are woven into the wool, not printed.

Wool Preparation

Before you begin any wool or wool felt project, you need to prepare the fabric. Preparing the wool gives it more loft as a result of the shrinkage that will occur. It also tightens the weave, which helps prevent fraying. Separate light from dark colors, just as for washing any other fabric. Most dark colors bleed to some degree. Put the wool into your washing machine and fill with hot water. No soap or detergent is necessary, but you may use a small amount if you prefer. Use your machine's soak or very gentle setting and allow the wool to spin through the entire cycle. You can wash smaller pieces of wool in the sink or put them in a mesh laundry bag and then in the washing machine.

Transfer wool to the dryer and use medium heat or the permanent-press setting. This will help soften the fabric, as opposed to just letting it air dry. When drying small pieces, toss an old towel in with them to prevent the wool pieces from forming a ball. Let the wool tumble until almost dry, and then remove it from the machine promptly to avoid any wrinkles.

Wool Appliqué by Hand

The projects that are made completely of wool (wool-on-wool) use different cutting and sewing techniques than those made with cotton. I always hand appliqué the shapes in wool-on-wool projects.

Supplies
In addition to your regular sewing supplies, the following items will help you achieve good results with your wool appliqué projects:

- Freezer paper
- Fabric glue—stick or bottle
- 6-ply embroidery floss—commercial or hand-dyed
- Embroidery or chenille needle

Cutting the Appliqué Shapes
When cutting wool shapes for hand appliqué, use freezer paper to create the templates.

1. Using the patterns provided with the projects, trace around the shapes on the paper side of the freezer paper. You should be able to easily see the black lines of the shapes through the paper. Rough cut around each shape but not on the drawn line.

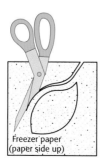

Freezer paper
(paper side up)

2. Iron the waxed (shiny) side of the freezer paper onto the prepared wool. Cut out the shapes on the drawn line.

3. Remove the freezer paper and refer to the project photo as well as any diagrams to position the shapes on the background fabric. These freezer-paper shapes may be used multiple times, which is helpful when you need more than one of the same shape.

4. To secure the shapes to the background fabric, put a small amount of fabric glue on the back of each piece. Try to avoid putting glue exactly at the edges, to ensure that your needle will glide through easily when you are stitching.

Embroidery Stitches
I used the stitches described here for the hand embroidery on wool-on-wool projects in this book. The stitches all use two strands of 6-ply embroidery floss.

1. To stitch the edges of most shapes, use a traditional buttonhole or blanket stitch.

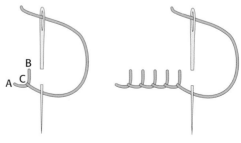

Blanket stitch

2. For stems and vines, use a ladder stitch. Stitch up through the background fabric next to the edge of the stem or vine. Stitch down through the

stem, placing the needle about halfway across the width of the stem. (Note: If the stem is quite wide, keep your stitch no longer than ¼".) Drop down ¼" under the fabric and bring the needle up at the edge of the stem on the opposite side. Repeat as you alternate sides to complete stitching the stem or vine.

Ladder stitch

3. For the center dots on wool pennies and also on "Fruit Salad Wall Hanging" on page 63, use a stitch that looks like a wagon wheel. Bring the needle up next to the edge of the dot and stitch back down in the center. Move directly across the dot from the first stitch and repeat. Keep stitching in this manner to evenly divide the dot into sections. Then stitch several French knots in the center to complete the embroidery.

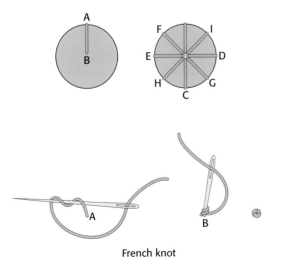

French knot

4. To create embroidered stems or to stitch letters, use a stem stitch.

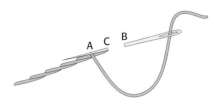

Stem stitch

HOW TO TRANSFER LETTERING TO FABRIC

To transfer letters and designs for embroidery, use a light box. First, place the pattern on the light box and secure it with tape so that it doesn't shift. Next, position the fabric in the correct place over the pattern. Trace the lines onto the fabric using a mechanical pencil for light fabrics and a white marking pencil for dark fabrics.

Wool and Cotton Appliqué by Machine

When sewing wool or cotton appliqué shapes to cotton background fabric, I use fusible-appliqué techniques and machine stitching. Fusing the appliqué shapes in place helps to prevent shifting while sewing. Use a lightweight fusible-web product so that your machine stitching is easier to accomplish. Fusible-web products with heavier glue may cause drag on the needle, resulting in skipped stitches.

Since fusible-web techniques require tracing *nonsymmetrical* patterns in reverse, the patterns for these shapes have been provided for you already reversed. When a project instructs you to cut a few patterns reversed, just cut the reverse of what is shown.

Supplies

In addition to your regular sewing supplies, you'll need the following items when creating wool-on-cotton or cotton-on-cotton projects:

- Lightweight fusible web
- Topstitch needles—size 12 for cotton-on-cotton and size 14 for wool-on-cotton
- Cotton machine-quilting thread—40-weight for cotton-on-cotton
- Cordonnet thread—30-weight for wool-on-cotton

Fusible Appliqué

Using your preferred fusible-web product, refer to the following steps to create perfect fusible-appliqué shapes.

1. Using the patterns provided with the projects, trace the appliqué shapes with a pencil onto the paper side of the fusible web. Since fusible web can be used only once, trace each shape as many times as needed for your chosen project.

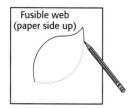

2. Rough cut the shapes from the fusible web, leaving approximately ¼" around the drawn line.

3. Press to fuse the shapes onto the wrong side of your appliqué fabric, following the manufacturer's instructions.

4. After allowing the fabric to cool, cut out the appliqué shapes on the drawn line. Peel the paper from the fabric.

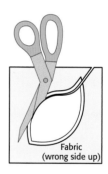

5. Refer to the project photo as well as any diagrams to position the shapes on the background fabric. Press to fuse the shapes in place.

6. Use a machine blanket or buttonhole stitch to secure the edges of the appliqué shapes.

Quiltmaking Tips

I n this section we'll discuss borders, ways to customize the projects in this book, and methods for finishing your quilts successfully.

Adding Borders

When border strips need to be pieced together for length, join the strips with a diagonal seam. This is stronger and nicer looking than a straight seam. Sew strips together by placing one strip right side up. Place another strip right side down, perpendicular to the first strip. Sew from corner to corner. Trim the extra fabric, leaving a ¼" seam allowance, and press the seam open.

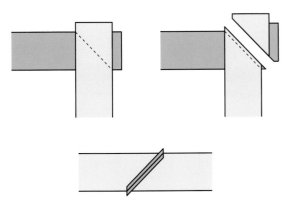

1. Measure the quilt top through the center from top to bottom and cut two border strips to that measurement. Sew the strips to the side edges of the quilt top. Press toward the border strips.

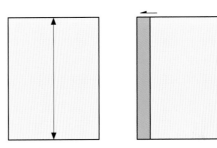

Measure the vertical center.

2. Measure the quilt top through the center from side to side, including the borders that you just added. Cut two strips to that measurement. Sew the strips to the top and bottom of the quilt top. Press toward the border strips.

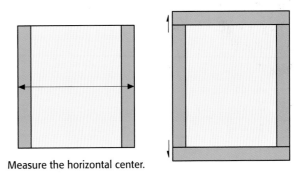

Measure the horizontal center.

Borders with Corner Squares

For borders that include corner squares, follow step 1 above to add the side borders, but then measure the quilt through the center from side to side *without* including the borders you just added. Add ½" to the measurement and cut two strips to the revised measurement. The project instructions will tell you the proper measurements for the corner squares. Sew a corner square to each end of the top and bottom border strips. Press the seams toward the strips. Sew the border strips to the quilt top, matching the seams. Press toward the border strips.

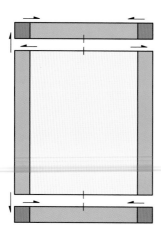

Scalloped Borders

Scalloped borders give a unique decorative look to a quilt. The following steps will help you create this type of border, such as the one I used on "Spring Is Sprung Quilt" on page 32 and "Star-Spangled Lap Quilt" on page 68. I wait to cut the scallops until after the quilt has been quilted. This helps prevent any stretching that may occur along the scalloped edge during the quilting process. Once the edges of the quilt have been trimmed and squared, you can begin to plan the scallops.

1. After sewing border strips to the quilt, decide how deep you'd like the scallops to be along the edges. Mark the borders to that depth using a removable marker such as a chalk pencil.

2. Mark a 45° diagonal line across one corner of the border as shown. Use a compass and template plastic to make a circle template, or simply use a circular object such as a plate that properly fits the corner. Center the template or plate in the corner. Trace around the curve of the circle with a fabric marking pen or pencil. Repeat for all four corners.

3. Measure the distance between the corner scallop marks along the top and bottom borders. Divide by the number of scallops that you'd like along the edge. Mark the edges of the quilt with pins at these intervals.

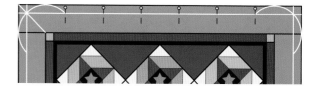

4. Using the circle template or plate, trace a curve at each interval between the pins to mark the scallops.

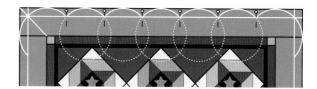

5. Repeat steps 3 and 4 for the side borders. The scallop measurement for the side borders might not be exactly the same as for the top and bottom borders, but a slight difference will be OK. Once scallops have been marked, cut along the traced lines.

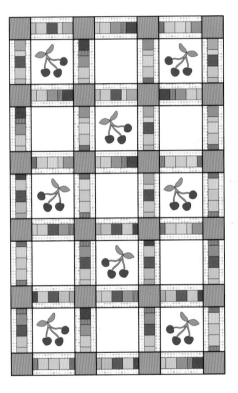

Project Variations

Here are some simple ways to create multiple variations of the projects in this book:

Adding or subtracting blocks can change a project to fit your own needs. For many of my projects, I begin with the design in mind rather than the use of the finished project. Adjusting sashing and borders will help you personalize most of these projects.

Using the appliqué designs from other projects is an easy way to completely change the look of a piece.

Using a copy machine, you can adjust the sizes of appliqué motifs to fit any project, large or small. You might also choose to add appliqué to empty borders or other blank spaces in a design.

Although the fabrics for these projects were selected to reflect a particular season, it is easy to change them to make a nonseasonal project. When picking fabrics for a project, I try to imagine a mood or theme for the quilt. This helps me be consistent in my fabric choices and stay away from selections that would detract from that mood. For example, in "Star-Spangled Lap Quilt" I wanted to maintain a vintage, Victorian feel.

Have fun creating your quilts!

Finishing the Quilt

The only projects in this book that use batting are those involving cotton fabrics; the wool-on-wool projects do not need any batting. Please use your preferred type of batting for the projects that require it. Many people choose their batting based on whether the quilting will be done by hand or by machine.

When cotton backing needs to be pieced together, the specific project instructions will indicate the number of fabric widths needed. The direction of the seam placement is also noted for rectangular quilts.

Straight-Grain Binding

I use 2¼"-wide strips for the binding on my projects. Straight-grain binding, cut from the crosswise grain, is used for most of the projects in this book. Cut the number of strips specified in the project instructions, and sew the strips together end to end using a diagonal seam. Trim the seam to ¼" and press open.

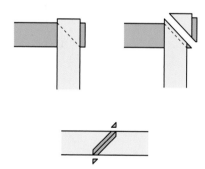

Bias Binding

For quilts with scalloped borders, you'll need to cut bias binding. This type of binding has more stretch and therefore accommodates the curves of the scallops.

1. Cut a square from the binding fabric. The exact size of the square is given in the project instructions. Place a pin in the middle of the square's top and bottom edges. Cut the square in half diagonally.

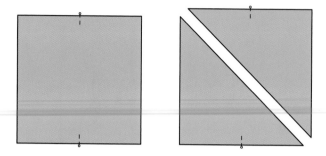

2. With the triangles right sides together, align the raw edges of the pinned sides and pin them together. Sew a ¼" seam. Remove the pins and press open.

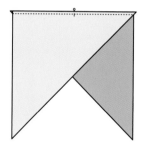

3. Mark cutting lines parallel to the *long* bias edges, spacing the lines 2¼" apart.

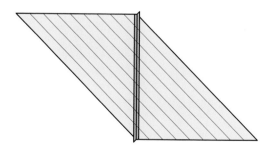

4. With right sides together, align the raw edges of the *short* sides of the shape. Offset one width of binding strip and pin. Sew with a ¼" seam and press open. This forms a tube.

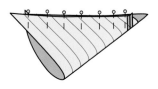

5. Begin cutting at the extended edge and follow the drawn lines to form one long binding strip.

Sewing Binding to the Quilt

1. Cut one end of the binding strip at a 45° angle. With wrong sides together, fold the strip in half lengthwise and press. Turn in the angled end ¼" and press.

2. Place the raw edges of the binding even with the raw edges of the quilt, starting at the center of the bottom edge. Start sewing 3" from the beginning of the binding strip. Sew the binding to the quilt using a ¼" seam allowance.

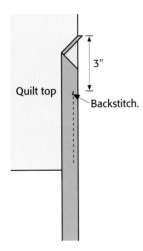

Quilt top

3"

Backstitch.

3. When you reach the first corner, stop sewing ¼" from the edge and backstitch. Remove the quilt from your machine.

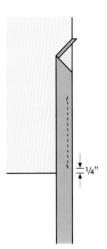

¼"

4. Rotate the quilt 90° and fold the binding strip up so that the edge of the strip is even with the edge of the quilt. Then fold the strip down, keeping the fold even with the edge of the quilt. Continue sewing, repeating this step at each corner.

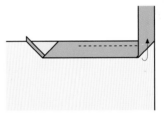

5. Stitch around the entire quilt, stopping about 6" from where you began. Remove the quilt from your machine. Trim the end of the binding, leaving at least ¼" extra. Tuck this into the beginning end of the binding, and finish sewing the binding to the quilt.

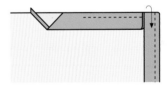

6. Turn the binding over to the back of the quilt and sew by hand using a small blind stitch.

Snowflake Lap Quilt

Designed and sewn by Julie Popa. Quilted by Paula Murray.

Let it snow while you are wrapped up and warm in this snuggly lap quilt. Even if you aren't in the mood for winter, this snowflake design would look beautiful in many other color schemes.

Finished Quilt: 58½" x 73½"
Finished Block: 12" x 12"

Materials

All yardages are based on 42"-wide fabric.

- 1½ yards of white print for blocks and inner border
- 1¼ yards of medium blue print #2 for outer border
- ⅞ yard of dark blue print #5 for middle border and binding
- ¾ yard of light blue print for blocks
- ⅝ yard of dark blue print #1 for nine-patch units, center squares of sashing, and border squares
- ½ yard of dark blue print #4 for sashing squares
- ⅜ yard of medium blue print #1 for nine-patch units
- ⅜ yard of dark blue print #2 for corner squares of blocks
- ⅜ yard of dark blue print #3 for corner squares of blocks
- ⅜ yard of cream-and-blue striped fabric for sashing
- 3¾ yards of fabric for backing (2 widths pieced horizontally)
- 64" x 79" piece of batting

Cutting

From dark blue print #1, cut:
- 5 strips, 2½" x 42"
- 1 strip, 3½" x 42"; crosscut into 6 squares, 3½" x 3½". Use the remainder of the strip to cut 4 squares, 2½" x 2½".

From medium blue print #1, cut:
- 4 strips, 2½" x 42"

From the white print, cut:
- 6 strips, 2⅜" x 42"; crosscut into 48 squares, 2⅜" x 2⅜". Cut each square once diagonally to yield 96 half-square triangles.
- 3 strips, 7¼" x 42"; crosscut into 12 squares, 7¼" x 7¼". Cut each square twice diagonally to yield 48 quarter-square triangles.
- 5 strips, 2½" x 42"

From the light blue print, cut:
- 9 strips, 2⅜" x 42"; crosscut into 144 squares, 2⅜" x 2⅜". Cut each square once diagonally to yield 288 half-square triangles.

From dark blue print #2, cut:
- 3 strips, 3½" x 42"; crosscut into 24 squares, 3½" x 3½"

From dark blue print #3, cut:
- 3 strips, 3½" x 42"; crosscut into 24 squares, 3½" x 3½"

From dark blue print #4, cut:
- 4 strips, 3½" x 42"; crosscut into 34 squares, 3½" x 3½"

From the cream-and-blue striped fabric, cut:
- 3 strips, 3½" x 42"; crosscut into 17 rectangles, 3½" x 6½"

From dark blue print #5, cut:
- 6 strips, 1½" x 42"
- 7 strips, 2¼" x 42"

From medium blue print #2, cut:
- 7 strips, 5½" x 42"

Making the Blocks

1. Sew a dark blue #1 strip to each long edge of a medium blue #1 strip to make strip set A. Press toward the dark blue strips. Make two strip sets. Cut 24 segments, 2½" wide.

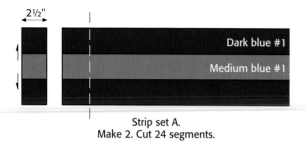

2½"

Dark blue #1

Medium blue #1

Strip set A.
Make 2. Cut 24 segments.

2. Sew a medium blue #1 strip to each long edge of the remaining dark blue #1 strip to make strip set B. Press toward the dark blue strip. Cut 12 segments, 2½" wide.

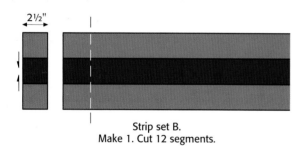

2½"

Strip set B.
Make 1. Cut 12 segments.

3. Sew together two segments from strip set A and one segment from strip set B to make a nine-patch unit; press in either direction. Make 12 nine-patch units.

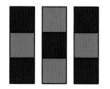

Make 12.

4. Sew a white 2⅜" triangle to a light blue 2⅜" triangle. Press toward the blue triangle. Make 96 half-square-triangle units.

Make 96.

5. Sew light blue 2⅜" triangles to the remaining sides of the white triangle in each of the units from step 4. Press toward the blue triangles. Make 96 units.

Make 96.

6. Sew triangle units from step 5 to both short sides of a white 7¼" triangle as shown. Press toward the corner units. Make 48 units.

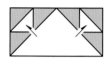

Make 48.

7. Sew a dark blue #2 square to each end of a unit from step 6. Press toward the dark blue squares. Make 12 rows. Make 12 additional rows using the dark blue #3 squares.

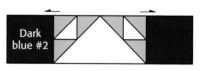

Dark blue #2

Make 12.

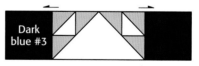

Dark blue #3

Make 12.

8. Sew two remaining units from step 6 to opposite sides of a nine-patch unit from step 3 as shown. Press toward the nine-patch unit. Make 12 rows.

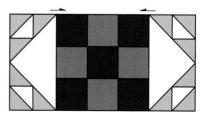

Make 12.

9. Sew two matching rows from step 7 to the top and bottom edges of a row from step 8. Press toward the outer rows. Make 12 blocks.

10. Sew a dark blue #4 square to each end of a cream-and-blue striped rectangle. Press toward the striped rectangle. Make 17 sashing units.

Make 17.

Quilt-Top Assembly

1. Referring to the quilt diagram, arrange and sew the blocks and sashing units into four rows. Press toward the sashing units.

2. Arrange and sew the remaining sashing units and the 3½" squares of dark blue #1 into three rows. Press toward the sashing units.

3. Sew the rows together, pressing toward the sashing units.

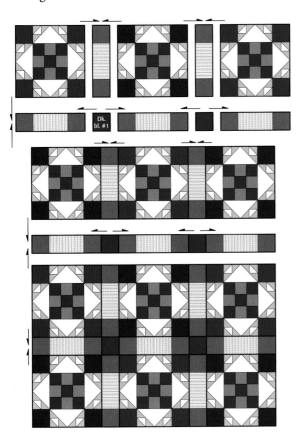

Adding the Borders

1. Sew the white strips together end to end and press. Refer to "Adding Borders" on page 9 to cut two side borders. Cut two borders for the top and bottom of the quilt, *not* including the measurement of the side borders.

2. Sew the border strips to the sides of the quilt top. Press toward the border strips.

3. Sew a 2½" square of dark blue #1 to both ends of the top and bottom border strips. Press toward the border strips. Sew to the top and bottom of the quilt top. Press toward the border strips.

4. Referring to "Adding Borders" on page 9, cut and sew the 1½" x 42" strips of dark blue #5 for the middle border and the 5½" x 42" strips of medium blue #2 for the outer border.

Finishing the Quilt

Layer and baste your quilt, and quilt as desired. Referring to "Straight-Grain Binding" on page 12, prepare the dark blue #5 binding and sew it to the quilt.

Warm Hearts Table Topper

Designed and sewn by Julie Popa. Quilted by Paula Murray.

Bring a little warmth into your winter with this cozy table topper.

Finished Quilt: 35⅛" x 35⅛"
Finished Block: 9" x 9"

Materials

Cotton yardages are based on 42"-wide fabric. Wool yardages are based on 54"-wide fabric.

- ½ yard of cream print for pieced border
- ½ yard of red print for inner border and border triangles
- ⅜ yard of white wool for snowflakes
- ⅜ yard of blue print #2 for pieced border
- ¼ yard of blue print #1 for pieced border
- ⅛ yard of yellow print for inner accent border
- 12" squares of 4 different blue fabrics for pieced blocks
- 10" x 10" square *each* of red and yellow wool for mittens
- Scraps of dark red wool for hearts on mittens
- Scraps of blue wool for cuffs on mittens
- ⅓ yard of blue print for binding
- 1¼ yards of fabric for backing
- 42" x 42" square of batting
- White embroidery floss for lettering

Cutting

From *each* of the 4 different blue fabrics, cut:
- 1 square, 10¼" x 10¼"; cut each square twice diagonally to yield 4 quarter-square triangles (16 total)

From the red print, cut:
- 2 strips, 2½" x 42"; cut in half crosswise to yield 4 strips, 2½" x 21"
- 2 squares, 7½" x 7½"; cut each square twice diagonally to yield 8 quarter-square triangles

From the yellow print, cut:
- 2 strips, 1¼" x 42"; cut in half crosswise to yield 4 strips, 1¼" x 21"

From blue print #1, cut:
- 1 square, 7½" x 7½"; cut twice diagonally to yield 4 quarter-square triangles

From blue print #2, cut:
- 2 strips, 5" x 42"; crosscut into 4 rectangles, 5" x 17⅞"

From the cream print, cut:
- 2 squares, 14⅛" x 14⅛"; cut each square once diagonally to yield 4 half-square triangles

From the blue print, cut:
- 4 strips, 2¼" x 42"

Making the Blocks

1. Sew two different blue 10¼" triangles together along the short sides as shown. Press the seam to one side. Repeat with two more triangles, making sure that you have used one triangle of each blue fabric. Sew these two units together to complete the block, and press. Repeat to make four blocks.

Make 4.

2. Referring to the photo on page 18, sew two blocks together and press the seam to one side. Repeat with the remaining two blocks, pressing the seam to the opposite side. Sew these two rows together and press.

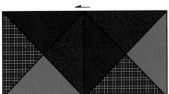

Quilt-Top Assembly

1. Sew a red strip to a yellow strip along the long edges. Press toward the red strip. Make four strip sets.

Make 4.

2. Using a rotary ruler marked with a 45° angle, cut one end of a strip set from step 1 at a 45° angle as shown. Measure 19¼" from the point of the angle and cut the other end at a 45° angle in the opposite direction to create a trapezoid shape. Make four units.

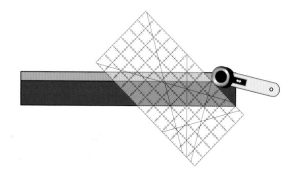

19¼"

Make 4.

3. Sew a unit from step 2 to each side of the center block unit. Press toward the strip units.

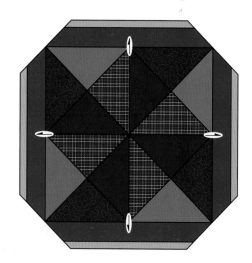

4. Sew a red triangle to each short side of a blue #1 triangle. Press toward the red triangles. Make four triangle units.

Make 4.

5. Sew a unit from step 4 to each side of the quilt center. Press toward the yellow accent border.

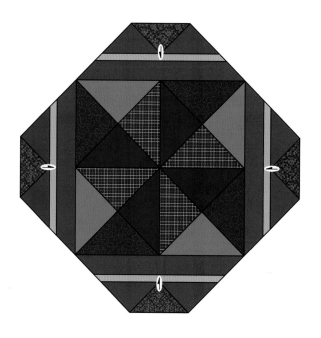

6. Cut the ends of a blue #2 rectangle at opposite 45° angles to create a trapezoid shape. Make four units.

Make 4.

7. Sew a unit from step 6 to each side of the quilt center. Press toward the blue trapezoid shapes.

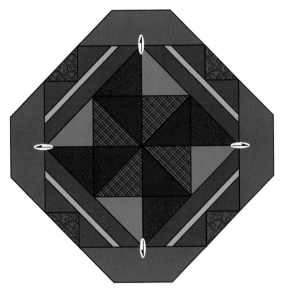

8. Sew a cream triangle to each side of the quilt center. Press toward the cream triangles.

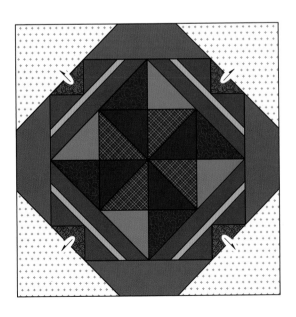

9. Refer to "Embroidery Stitches" on page 6 and the lettering patterns on page 22 to stitch the words onto the blue segments of the pieced border.

Appliqué

1. Refer to "Fusible Appliqué" on page 8 for specific appliqué instructions. Refer to the patterns on page 23 to cut the following from prepared wool:

   ◆ 2 mittens from *both* yellow and red wool
   ◆ 2 mittens *reversed* from *both* yellow and red wool
   ◆ 8 hearts from dark red wool
   ◆ 8 mitten cuffs from blue wool
   ◆ 4 snowflake centers from white wool
   ◆ 16 each of long and short snowflake branches from white wool
   ◆ 16 each of large and small snowflake tips from white wool

2. Refer to the photo on page 18 to arrange the appliqué shapes on the quilt top. Use the seams of the pieced blocks as a guide for positioning the snowflake pieces. Fuse the shapes in place and use a machine blanket stitch to secure the shapes to the quilt.

Finishing the Quilt

Layer and baste your quilt, and quilt as desired. Referring to "Straight-Grain Binding" on page 12, prepare the blue print binding and sew it to the quilt.

...Warm hearts

Cold hands...

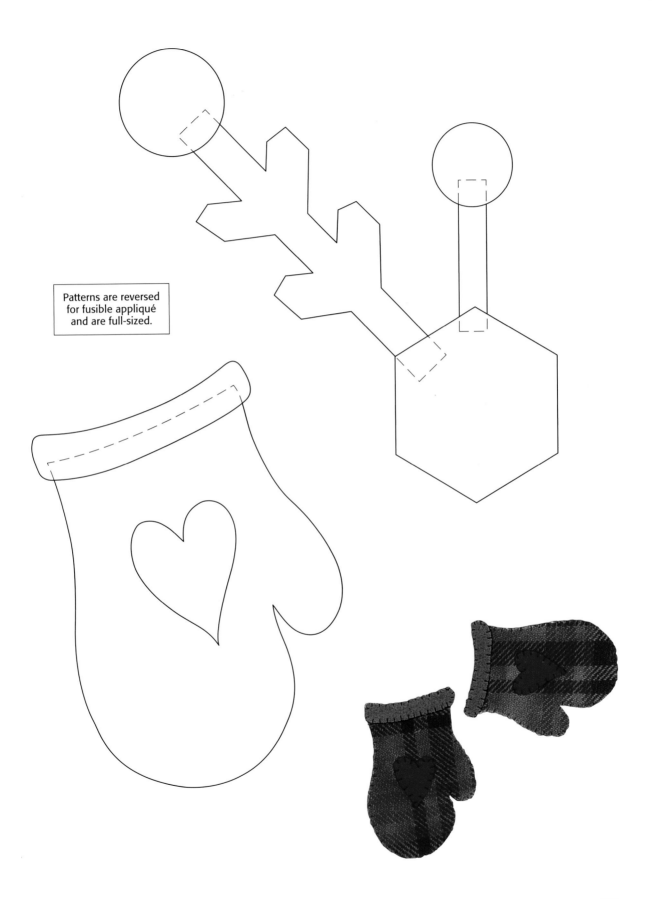

Patterns are reversed
for fusible appliqué
and are full-sized.

Be My Valentine Wall Hanging

Designed and sewn by Julie Popa. Quilted by Paula Murray.

This valentine quilt will brighten any home each winter. This project is simple and quick to piece.

Finished Quilt: 52½" x 55½"

Materials

Cotton yardages are based on 42"-wide fabric. Wool yardages are based on 54"-wide fabric.

◆ 1¾ yards *total* of assorted red prints for pieced blocks and pieced outer borders
◆ 1⅓ yards of cream print for appliqué background
◆ ½ yard of tan print for inner border
◆ ⅜ yard *total* of assorted red and pink wool for appliquéd hearts
◆ ¼ yard of black wool for appliquéd vine
◆ Assorted scraps of green wool for leaves
◆ ½ yard of dark red print for binding
◆ 3½ yards of fabric for backing (2 widths pieced vertically)
◆ 59" x 62" piece of batting

Cutting

From the assorted red prints, cut:
◆ 1 strip, 2½" x 42"
◆ 1 strip, 3½" x 42"
◆ 20 rectangles, 2½" x 7½"
◆ 10 rectangles, 1½" x 7½"
◆ 16 squares, 5½" x 5½"
◆ 2½"-wide strips of various lengths to equal 200"
◆ 1½"-wide strips of various lengths to equal 200"
◆ 4 squares, 3½" x 3½"

From the cream print, cut:
◆ 3 rectangles, 8½" x 41½", from the length of the fabric

From the tan print, cut:
◆ 5 strips, 3" x 42"

From the dark red print, cut:
◆ 6 strips, 2¼" x 42"

Making the Pieced Red Rectangles

1. Sew the red 2½" x 42" strip to the red 3½" x 42" strip along the long edges to make a strip set. Press the seam allowance to one side. Cut two segments, 7½" wide.

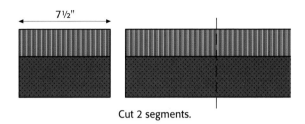

7½"

Cut 2 segments.

2. Sew together two red 2½" x 7½" rectangles and one red 1½" x 7½" rectangle as shown. Press all seam allowances in the same direction. Make 10 units.

Make 10.

Quilt-Top Assembly

1. Referring to the diagram below, arrange strip set segments, 7½" units, and red 5½" squares in four rows. Note that each row begins and ends with a red square. Sew the units into rows and press toward the red squares.

2. Sew a cream rectangle between each pieced row and press toward the pieced rows.

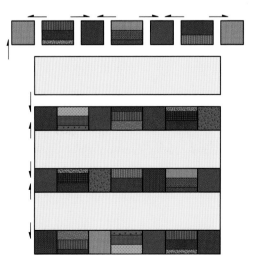

Appliqué

1. Refer to "Fusible Appliqué" on page 8 for specific appliqué instructions. Refer to the patterns on pages 27–29 to cut the following from prepared wool:

   - 2 *each* of hearts A–E from assorted red and pink wool
   - 1 *each* of hearts A–E *reversed* from assorted red and pink wool
   - 2 of heart B2 from pink wool
   - 1 of heart B2 *reversed* from pink wool
   - 2 each of vines A–E from black wool
   - 1 each of vines A–E *reversed* from black wool
   - 24 leaves from green wool

2. Refer to the photo on page 24 to position the appliqué shapes on the quilt top. Fuse the shapes in place and use a machine blanket stitch to secure the shapes to the quilt.

Adding the Borders

1. Sew the tan strips together end to end and press. Refer to "Adding Borders" on page 9 to cut and sew the inner border.

2. Sew the red 2½"-wide strip lengths together end to end and press. Using the measuring method described in "Adding Borders," cut two side borders. Cut two borders for the top and bottom of the quilt, *not* including the side borders.

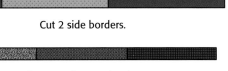

Cut 2 side borders.

Cut 2 top/bottom borders.

3. Repeat step 2 using the red 1½"-wide strips.

4. Sew together a side border strip of each width and press toward the 2½" border. Repeat.

5. Sew together a top or bottom border strip of each width and press toward the 2½" border. Repeat.

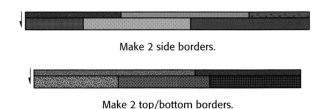

Make 2 side borders.

Make 2 top/bottom borders.

6. Sew the side borders to the quilt top, placing the 2½" borders toward the center of the quilt. Press toward the pieced red border.

7. Sew a red 3½" square to each end of the remaining border strips. Press toward the strips.

Make 2.

8. Sew the border strips to the top and bottom of the quilt top, placing the 2½" borders toward the quilt center. Press toward the red border.

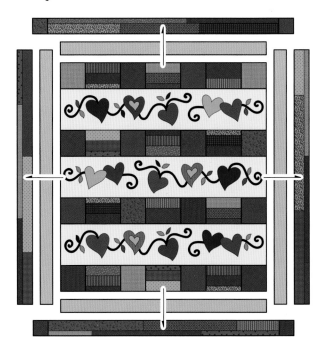

Finishing the Quilt

Layer and baste your quilt, and quilt as desired. Referring to "Straight-Grain Binding" on page 12, prepare the dark red binding and sew it to the quilt.

Enlarge patterns 110%.
Patterns are reversed
for fusible appliqué.

Vine A

Heart A

Heart B

Heart B2

Vine B

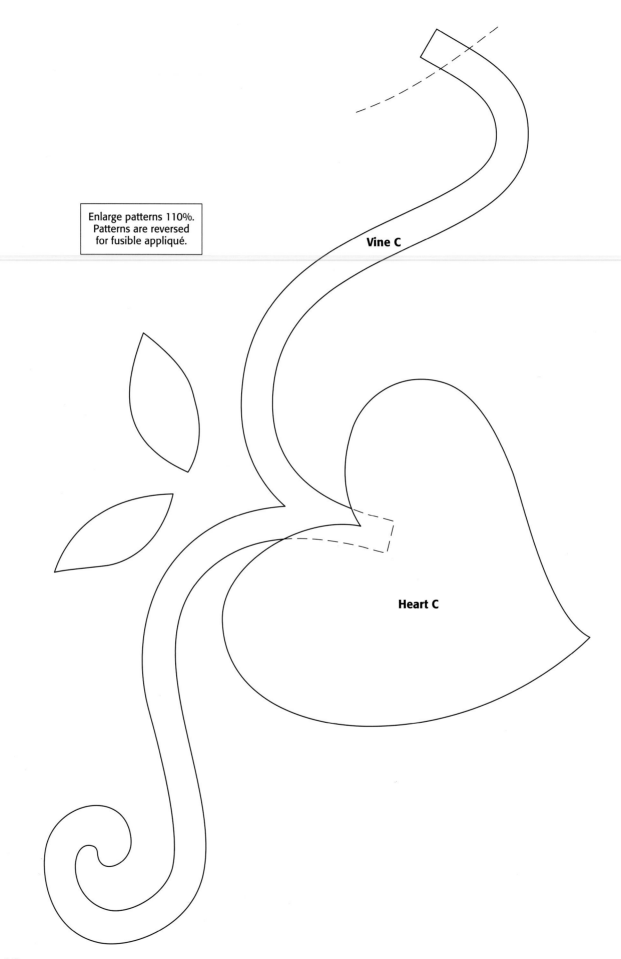

Enlarge patterns 110%.
Patterns are reversed
for fusible appliqué.

Vine C

Heart C

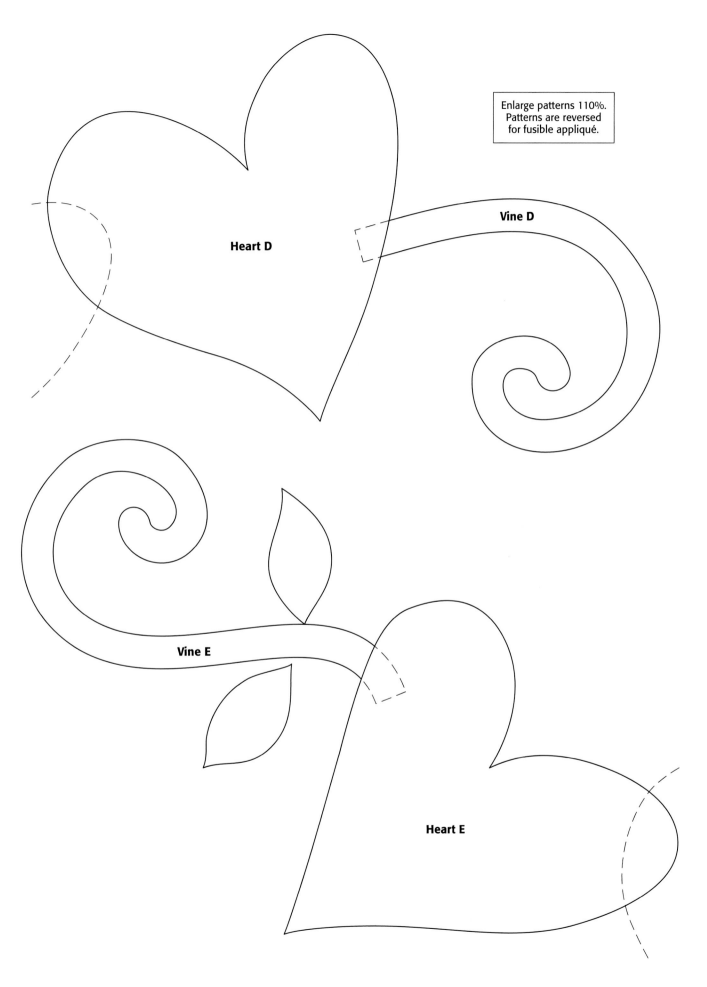

Enlarge patterns 110%.
Patterns are reversed
for fusible appliqué.

Heart D

Vine D

Vine E

Heart E

Heartfelt Wool Table Runner

Designed by Julie Popa. Hand sewn by Yvonne Fonnesbeck and Bette Popa.

Make this lighthearted project to brighten your table for the season of love. This project can be made quickly when you want to "give your heart" to one of your favorite valentines!

Finished Project: 9½" x 52"

Materials

Wool yardages are based on 54"-wide fabric.

- 1¾ yards of pink wool for small tongues, hearts, and backing
- ⅜ yard of tan wool for background
- ¼ yard of red wool for large tongues and one heart
- ¼ yard of black wool for vines
- ⅛ yard of dark red wool for one heart and dots on tongues
- Two 5" squares of red wool for hearts
- Assorted scraps of green wool for leaves
- Embroidery floss to match background and wool appliqués

Cutting

From the prepared tan wool, cut:
- 1 rectangle, 10" x 41"

Appliqué

1. Refer to "Wool Appliqué by Hand" on page 6 for specific appliqué instructions. Refer to the patterns on pages 27–29 and page 31 to cut the following from prepared wool:

    - 1 *each* of hearts A–E from red, dark red, and pink wool (5 hearts total)
    - 1 of heart B2 from pink wool
    - 1 *each* of vines A–E from black wool
    - 8 leaves from green wool
    - 6 small tongues from pink wool (Note: Cut these along one *long* edge of the wool to preserve the length of the yardage for backing.)
    - 6 large tongues from red wool
    - 6 dots for tongues from dark red wool

2. Sew the appliqués of hearts and leaves to the tan background rectangle using the blanket stitch. Sew the appliqués of vines using the ladder stitch.

3. Sew a dark red dot to a small pink tongue using a blanket stitch. Make six small appliquéd tongues.

4. Sew a pink appliquéd tongue to a large red tongue using a blanket stitch. Make six large appliquéd tongues.

Making the Project

1. Fold each edge of the appliquéd tan rectangle under a generous ½" and press all around.

2. Lay the tan rectangle on top of the remainder of the pink wool, allowing for at least 1" of pink on each side. Insert a tongue so that ½" of the straight end is tucked between the tan wool and the pink wool as shown. Position three tongues at each end of the runner and pin in place.

3. Using a blanket stitch, sew around the edges of the tan wool rectangle as well as the edges of each tongue.

4. Trim around all edges of the pink wool, leaving a generous ¼" border. Cut between each tongue, stopping where the tongues meet the tan wool.

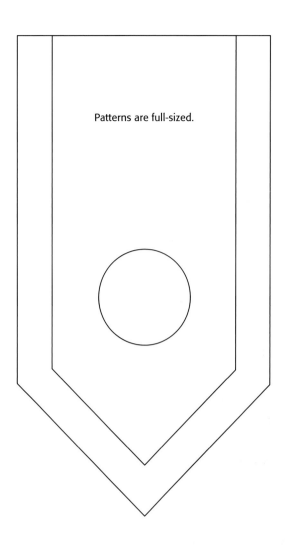

Patterns are full-sized.

Spring Is Sprung Quilt

Designed and sewn by Julie Popa. Quilted by Paula Murray.

Finished Quilt: 77½" x 107"
Finished Block: 14" x 14"

Materials

All yardages are based on 42"-wide fabric.

- 2⅛ yards of green floral for outer border
- 2⅛ yards of cream dot print for sashing
- 1⅞ yards *total* of assorted pastel prints (pink, purple, yellow, and green) for blocks and pieced setting triangles
- 1⅝ yards *total* of assorted green prints for vine, stem, and leaf appliqués
- 1¼ yards of blue print for block frames and inner border
- 1¼ yards of yellow dot print for sashing squares and setting triangles
- 1 yard of white print for background of appliqué blocks
- Assorted scraps of pink, blue, yellow, orange, and purple fabrics for flower appliqués
- 1⅛ yards of pink fabric for bias binding
- 7 yards of fabric for backing (3 widths pieced horizontally)
- 84" x 113" piece of batting

Cutting

From the white print, cut:
- 7 squares, 10⅜" x 10⅜"

From the assorted pastel prints, cut:
- 28 squares, 4⅜" x 4⅜"; cut these in 7 sets of 4 matching squares per set. Cut each square once diagonally to yield 56 half-square triangles.
- 28 squares, 4" x 4"; cut these in 7 sets of 4 matching squares per set.
- 30 squares, 5¾" x 5¾"

From the blue print, cut:
- 14 strips, 1⅜" x 42"; crosscut into 14 rectangles, 1⅜" x 14½", and 14 rectangles, 1⅜" x 16¼"
- 8 strips, 2¼" x 42"

From the cream dot print, cut:
- 12 strips, 5¾" x 42"; crosscut into 24 rectangles, 5¾" x 16¼"

From the yellow dot print, cut:
- 2 strips, 5¾" x 42"; crosscut into 8 squares, 5¾" x 5¾"
- 3 strips, 8⅝" x 42"; crosscut into 9 squares, 8⅝" x 8⅝". Cut each square twice diagonally to yield 36 quarter-square triangles. Use the remainder of a strip to cut 2 squares, 4⅝" x 4⅝"; cut each square once diagonally to yield 4 half-square triangles.

From the green floral, cut:
- 9 strips, 7½" x 42"

Appliqué

1. Refer to "Fusible Appliqué" on page 8 for specific appliqué instructions. Refer to the patterns on pages 36–40 to cut the following:
   - 1 iris from dark purple
   - 1 iris from light purple
   - 6 iris centers from yellow
   - 1 iris leaf from dark green
   - 1 iris leaf from light green
   - 4 tulip petals from dark pink
   - 4 tulip petals from light pink
   - 4 tulip dots from yellow
   - 2 tulip leaves from green
   - 6 daffodil petals from yellow
   - 6 daffodil cups from orange
   - 6 daffodil crowns from dark orange
   - 2 sets of daffodil leaves from green
   - 10 lily of the valley flowers from a variety of blues
   - 1 lily of the valley large leaf from dark green
   - 2 lily of the valley leaf accents from light green
   - 1 lily of the valley *reversed* large leaf from light green
   - 2 lily of the valley *reversed* leaf accents from dark green
   - 24 vines from dark green
   - 48 vine leaves from dark green
   - 24 vine leaves from light green

2. Fuse the floral appliqués to the white background squares, placing the bottoms of leaves and stems directly on the cut edges of the squares. The seam allowance will be sewn through the appliqué. Make seven blocks.

3. Fuse the leaf and vine appliqués to the cream dot rectangles. Make 24 sashing units.

4. Use a machine blanket stitch to secure the appliqué shapes in place.

Making the Blocks

1. Sew matching pastel print 4⅜" triangles to two adjacent sides of a 4" square of a different pastel print as shown. Press toward the triangles. Make four units of the same color combination for one block. Vary the colors for the next block. Make 28 units total.

Make 28
in sets of four.

2. Fold one floral appliqué block in half and crease within the seam allowances on two opposite sides to mark the centers. Fold the block in the opposite direction to mark the remaining sides. With right sides together, sew a matching unit from step 1 to each side of one floral appliqué block as shown, matching the centers of the blocks with the seam point of the pieced unit. Press toward the pieced units. Make seven blocks.

Make 7.

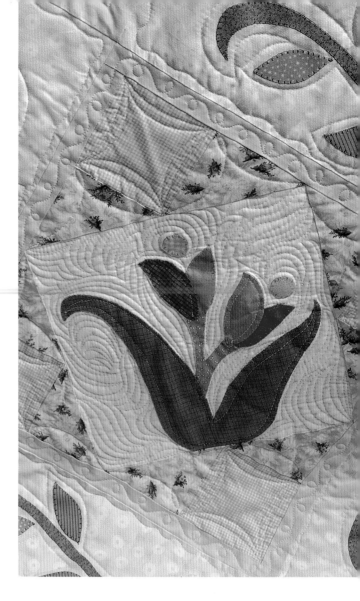

3. Sew blue 1⅜" x 14½" rectangles to opposite sides of an appliqué block. Press toward the blue rectangles. Sew blue 1⅜" x 16¼" rectangles to the remaining sides of the block. Press toward the blue rectangles. Repeat for each block.

Make 7.

4. Sew yellow dot 8⅝" triangles to two adjacent sides of a pastel print 5¾" square. Press toward the triangles. Make 10 units.

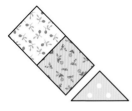

Make 10.

5. Sew two pastel print 5¾" squares and one yellow dot 8⅝" triangle together as shown. Press the seams in opposite directions. Make 10 units.

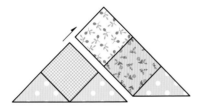

Make 10.

6. Sew one unit from step 4 to one unit from step 5 as shown; press. Make 10 setting triangles.

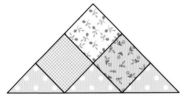

Make 10.

Quilt-Top Assembly

1. Refer to the quilt diagram to arrange the following blocks and units into diagonal rows: seven appliqué blocks, 24 sashing units, eight yellow 5¾" squares, six yellow 8⅝" side setting triangles, 10 pieced setting triangles, and four yellow 4⅝" corner triangles.

2. Sew the blocks and units into three block rows, four sashing rows, and two corner rows. Press toward the sashing units.

3. Sew the rows together, adding the yellow corner triangles last. Press toward the sashing rows.

Adding the Borders

1. Sew the blue 2¼" x 42" strips together end to end and press. Refer to "Adding Borders" on page 9 to cut and sew the inner border.

2. Repeat step 1 using the green floral strips for the outer border.

3. Mark and cut scallops, if desired, referring to "Scalloped Borders" on page 10.

Finishing the Quilt

Layer and baste your quilt, and quilt as desired. Refer to "Bias Binding" on page 12 to cut a 34" square from the pink fabric. Prepare the binding and sew it to the quilt.

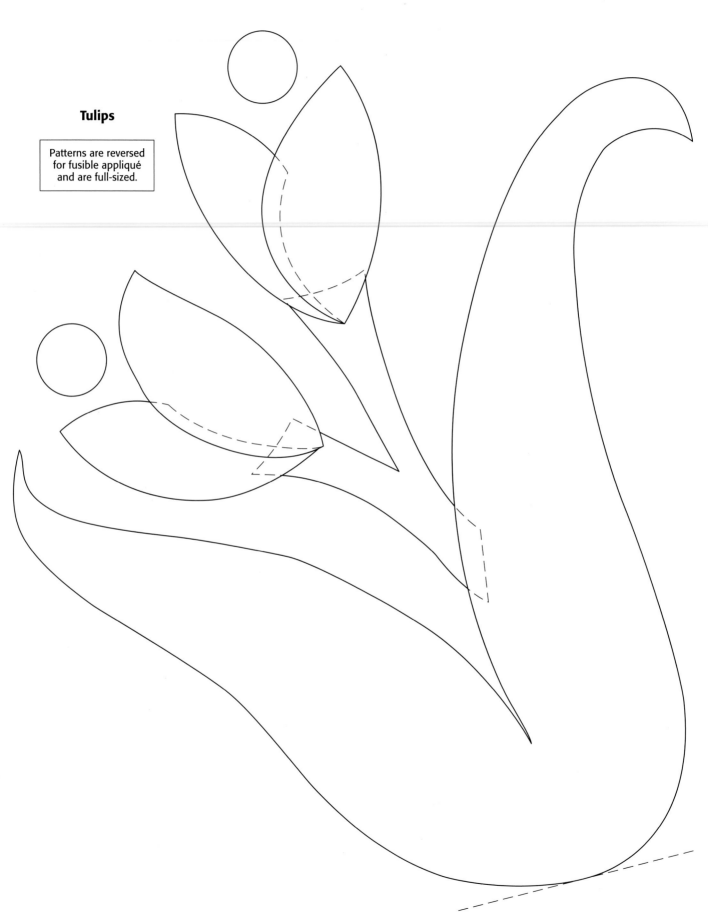

Tulips

Patterns are reversed
for fusible appliqué
and are full-sized.

Lily of the valley

Patterns are reversed
for fusible appliqué
and are full-sized.

Daffodils

Patterns are reversed for fusible appliqué and are full-sized.

Connect to leaf piece at lower right to complete pattern.

Connect to leaf piece at left to complete pattern.

Irises

Patterns are reversed
for fusible appliqué
and are full-sized.

Connect to leaf piece
on page 40
to complete pattern.

Patterns are reversed
for fusible appliqué
and are full-sized.

Connect to leaf piece
on page 39
to complete pattern.

Spring Penny Rug

Designed by Julie Popa. Colors selected and rug sewn by Yvonne Fonnesbeck.

Stitch this penny rug to decorate with for the season. The rug's small size makes it a great travel project.

Finished Project: 14" diameter

Materials

Wool yardages are based on 54"-wide fabric.

- ⅜ yard of cream wool for background and pennies
- ⅜ yard of tan wool for backing and pennies
- 10" x 10" square of green wool for leaves
- Assorted scraps of pink, yellow, blue, green, and peach wool for flowers, stem, and center of pennies
- Embroidery floss to match appliqués

Cutting *(Patterns are on page 43.)*

From the prepared cream wool, cut:

- 1 large background circle
- 11 large pennies

From the prepared tan wool, cut:

- 1 large backing circle
- 33 large pennies

Appliqué

1. Refer to "Wool Appliqué by Hand" on page 6 for complete instructions. Refer to the patterns on page 43 to cut the following from prepared wool:

- 6 tulip petals from various shades of peach and pink wool
- 1 stem from medium green wool
- 2 leaves using 2 shades of lighter green wool
- 3 yellow flower centers
- 22 small pennies from various shades of pink, yellow, blue, light green, and peach wool

2. Refer to the photo on page 41 to arrange the appliqué shapes on the cream wool circle. Stitch the appliqués to the background using a blanket stitch. Add accent stitching to the leaves.

Making the Project

1. Sew the tan wool circle to the back of the cream wool circle using a hand blanket stitch around the edges.

Sew front to back.

2. Make pennies by sewing a small penny to a large penny with the stitch shown. Refer to "Embroidery Stitches" on page 6 for instructions. Make 11 cream pennies and 11 tan pennies.

3. Sew the remaining large tan pennies to the back of the stitched pennies with a blanket stitch around the edges. Make 22 pennies.

4. Lay out the entire project on a flat surface with the pennies touching the center circle and each other as shown. Pin in place.

5. Using regular sewing thread (cotton or silk), take several stitches to connect the pennies to each other and to the center circle.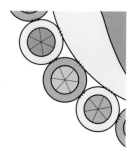

Stitching line

Enlarge tulip patterns 150%.
Penny patterns are full-sized.

Iris Wool Table Runner

Designed and sewn by Julie Popa

Make these iris blooms to enjoy before your outdoor garden springs to life. This simple table runner will add lasting beauty to any room.

Finished Project: 17" x 46"

Materials

Wool yardages are based on 54"-wide fabric. Wool felt yardage is based on 36"-wide fabric.

- 1½ yards of purple wool felt for backing
- ½ yard of cream wool for background
- ¼ yard of light green wool for leaves and stems
- ¼ yard of medium green wool for leaves and stems
- Assorted scraps of light, medium, and dark purple wool for iris flowers and yellow for iris centers
- Embroidery floss to match wool background and appliqués
- Freezer paper for pattern

Cutting

From the prepared cream wool, cut:
1 rectangle, 15" x 43"

Appliqué

1. Refer to "Wool Appliqué by Hand" on page 6 for specific appliqué instructions. Refer to the patterns on page 46 to cut the following from prepared wool:

    - 6 iris petals from various shades of purple wool
    - 18 iris centers from yellow wool
    - 2 iris buds from purple wool
    - 2 large iris leaves from light green wool
    - 2 large iris leaves *reversed* from medium green wool
    - 4 single stems from light green wool
    - 2 double stems from medium green wool

2. Refer to the photo above to position the appliqué shapes on the cream background. Sew the appliqué shapes in place using a blanket stitch.

Preparing the Backing

1. Cut a 20" x 47" rectangle from freezer paper. Fold in half both vertically and horizontally.

2. Creating template B using the pattern on page 48, place the edge of the template along the center fold lines of the freezer paper as shown. Trace around the template, including the scallops. Repeat to trace template B twice within each of the four sections of freezer paper.

3. Creating template A using the pattern on page 47, match the edges of the template to the drawn lines of template B. Trace template A once within each freezer-paper section.

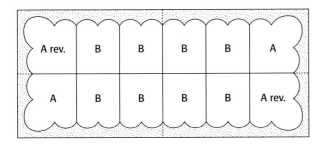

4. Press the freezer paper onto the purple wool felt and cut through both layers on the traced scallop line. Remove the freezer paper.

Making the Project

1. Fold under ½" on each edge of the appliquéd background rectangle and press all around.

2. Place the appliquéd top on the purple backing. Pin in place.

3. Using a blanket stitch, sew the edges of the cream rectangle to the purple backing. Try to catch just the top layers of the backing so that you don't stitch all the way through to the back of the purple wool felt.

Enlarge patterns 200%.

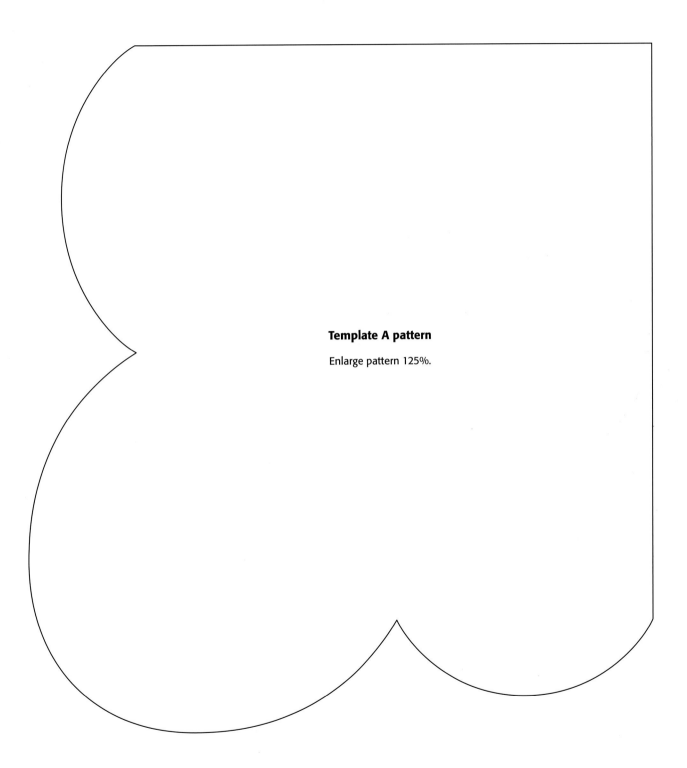

Template A pattern

Enlarge pattern 125%.

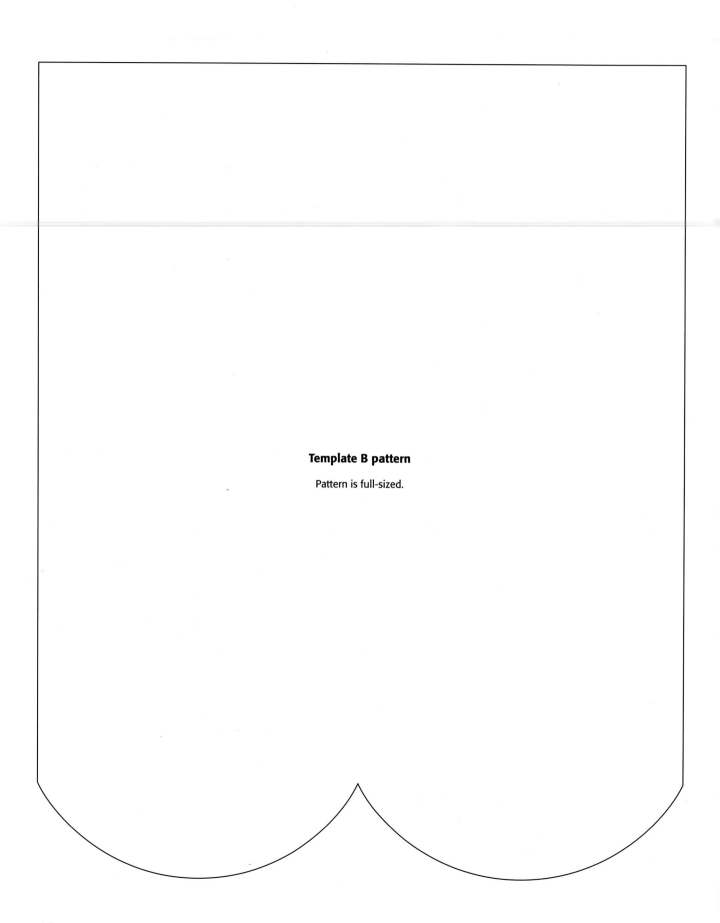

Template B pattern

Pattern is full-sized.

Spring Bouquet Table Topper

Designed and sewn by Julie Popa. Quilted by Paula Murray.

Freshly picked flowers always brighten a room. Make this bouquet to last the whole year through.

Finished Quilt: 35" x 35"
Finished Block: 9" x 9"

Materials

Cotton yardages are based on 42"-wide fabric. Wool yardages are based on 54"-wide fabric.

- ⅜ yard of bright yellow print for pieced outer border
- ⅜ yard of cream floral for pieced outer border
- ¼ yard of green plaid for inner border
- ¼ yard of red plaid for corner triangles
- ¼ yard of red checked fabric for corner squares
- ¼ yard of red wool for flowers
- ¼ yard of green wool for leaves
- ⅛ yard of dark red print for inner accent border
- 12" squares of 4 different cream and light yellow fabrics for pieced blocks
- 7" x 13" rectangle of yellow wool for bow
- ⅓ yard of light red print for binding
- 1⅓ yards of fabric for backing
- 40" x 40" square of batting
- Green embroidery floss for stems, assorted colors to match appliqués

Cutting

From *each* of the 4 different cream and light yellow fabrics, cut:
- 1 square, 10¼" x 10¼"; cut each square twice diagonally to yield 4 quarter-square triangles (16 total)

From the green plaid, cut:
- 2 strips, 2½" x 42"; cut in half crosswise to yield 4 strips, 2½" x 21"

From the dark red print, cut:
- 2 strips, 1¼" x 42"; cut in half crosswise to yield 4 strips, 1¼" x 21"

From the red plaid, cut:
- 1 strip, 5½" x 42"; crosscut into 4 squares, 5½" x 5½". Cut each square once diagonally to yield 8 half-square triangles.

From the red checked fabric, cut:
- 1 strip, 5" x 42"; crosscut into 4 squares, 5" x 5"

From the cream floral, cut:
- 2 strips, 5" x 42"; crosscut into 4 rectangles, 5" x 17⅞"

From the bright yellow print, cut:
- 2 strips, 5" x 42"; crosscut into 4 rectangles, 5" x 9¾", and 4 rectangles, 5" x 14¼"

From the light red print, cut:
- 4 strips, 2¼" x 42"

Making the Blocks

1. Sew two different cream and light yellow 10¼" triangles together along the short sides as shown. Press the seam to one side. Repeat with two more triangles, making sure that you have used one triangle of each cream and light yellow fabric. Sew these two units together to complete the block, and press. Repeat to make four blocks.

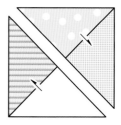

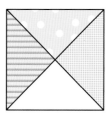

Make 4.

2. Referring to the photo on page 49 and the diagram on page 51, sew two blocks together and press the seam to one side. Repeat with the remain-

ing two blocks, pressing the seam to the opposite side. Sew these two rows together and press.

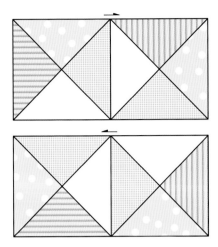

Quilt-Top Assembly

1. Sew a green plaid strip to a dark red strip along the long edges. Press toward the red strip. Make four strip sets.

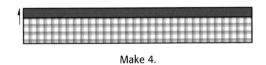

Make 4.

2. Using a rotary ruler marked with a 45° angle, cut one end of a strip set from step 1 at a 45° angle as shown. Measure 19¼" from the point of the angle and cut the other end at a 45° angle in the opposite direction to create a trapezoid shape. Make four units.

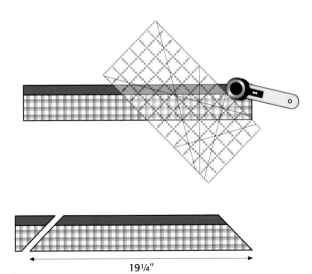

19¼"

Make 4.

3. Sew a unit from step 2 to each side of the center block unit. Press toward the strip units.

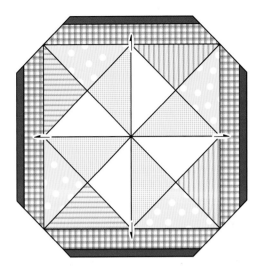

4. Sew red plaid triangles to two adjacent sides of a red checked square. Press toward the triangles. Make four units.

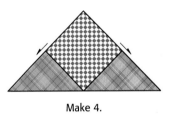

Make 4.

5. Sew a unit from step 4 to each side of the quilt center. Press toward the red strips.

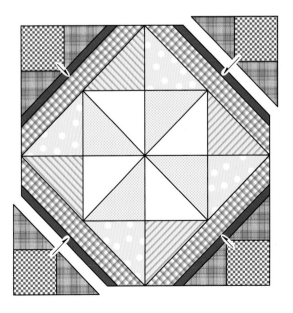

6. Cut the ends of a cream floral rectangle at opposite 45° angles to create a trapezoid shape. Make four units.

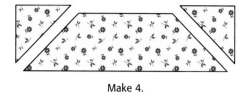

Make 4.

7. Place two bright yellow 5" x 9¾" rectangles together with right sides facing up. Place the remaining yellow 5" x 9¾" rectangles together with right sides *down* on top of the first two rectangles. You'll have four layers of fabric. Cut one end of the strips at a 45° angle as shown. Repeat using the yellow 5" x 14¼" rectangles.

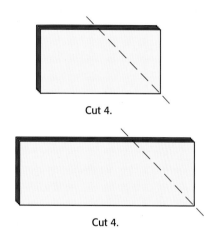

Cut 4.

Cut 4.

8. Sew a yellow 5" x 9¾" shape from step 7 to each end of a cream trapezoid from step 6. Press toward the yellow pieces. Make two border units. Repeat using the yellow 5" x 14¼" shapes.

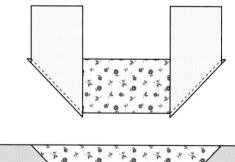

Make 2 short and 2 long.

9. Fold the two short border units from step 8 in half and crease to mark the center. Refer to "Adding Borders" on page 9 to trim and sew these borders to the top and bottom of the quilt top, matching the center of the border strips to the center of the quilt edges. Sew the long border units from step 8 to the side edges.

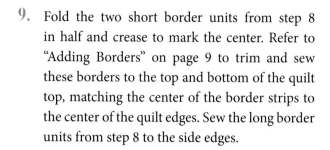

Crease

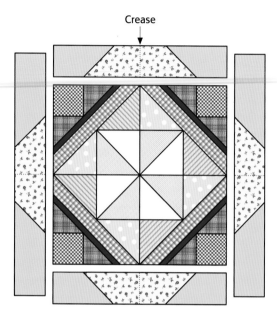

Appliqué

1. Refer to "Fusible Appliqué" on page 8 for specific appliqué instructions. Refer to the patterns on page 53 to cut the following from prepared wool:

   - 12 flowers from red wool
   - 10 of leaf A from green wool
   - 20 each of leaves B and C from green wool
   - 2 of leaf D from green wool
   - 4 of leaf E from green wool
   - 1 bow from yellow wool

2. Position the appliqué shapes on the quilt top. Fuse the shapes in place and use a machine blanket stitch to secure. Refer to the photo on page 49 and the diagram on page 54 for placement of the embroidered stems.

Finishing the Quilt

Layer and baste your quilt, and quilt as desired. Referring to "Straight-Grain Binding" on page 12, prepare the light red binding and sew it to the quilt.

Patterns are reversed
for fusible appliqué
and are full-sized.

Leaf A

Leaf B

Leaf C

Leaf D

Leaf E

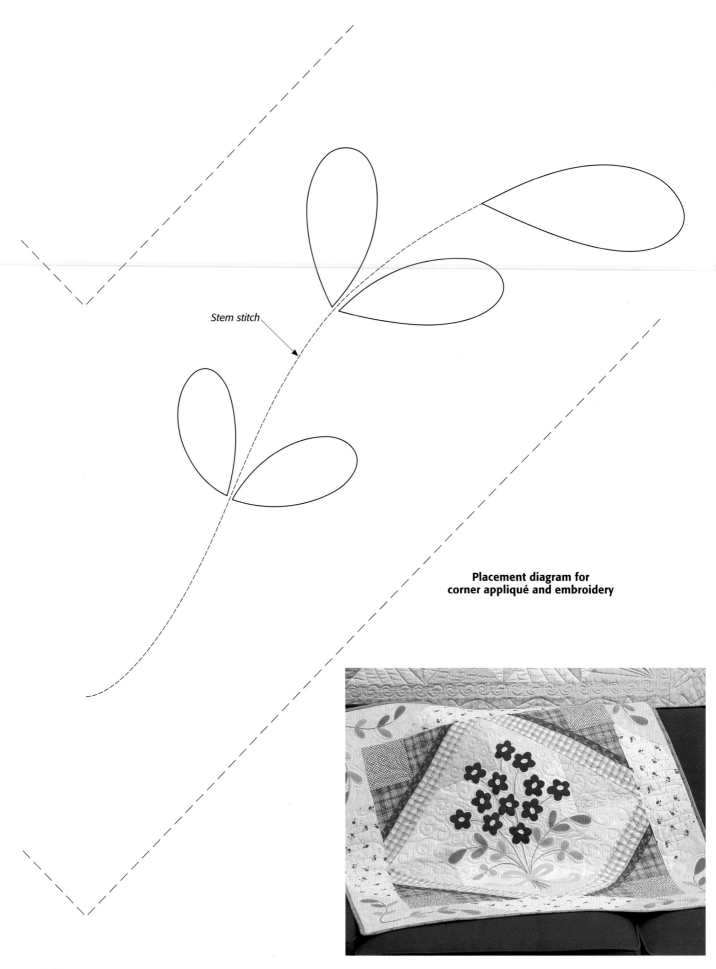

Stem stitch

**Placement diagram for
corner appliqué and embroidery**

Sunshine Lap Quilt

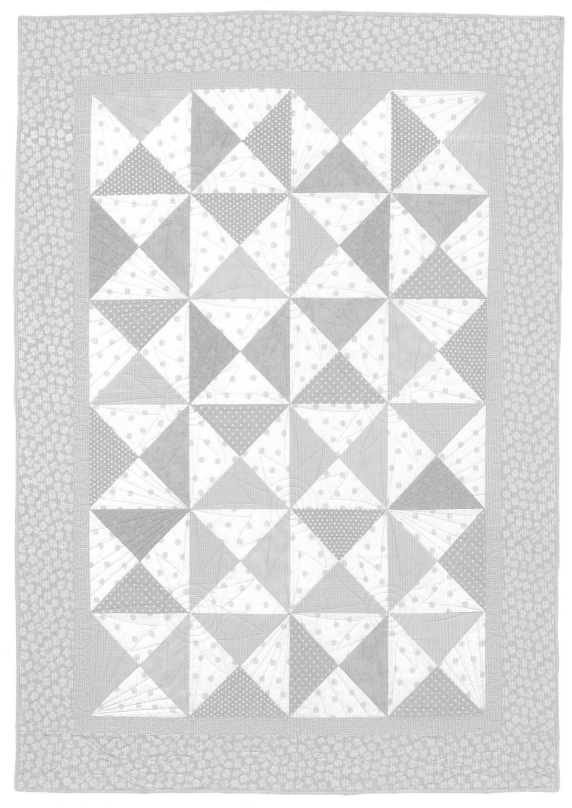

Designed and sewn by Julie Popa. Quilted by Paula Murray.

This lap quilt is great for a quick weekend project. It can be done as a two-color project as shown or in multiple colors.

Finished Quilt: 50½" x 68½"
Finished Block: 9" x 9"

Materials

All yardages are based on 42"-wide fabric.

- 1⅓ yards *total* of assorted yellow prints for blocks
- 1⅓ yards of cream print for blocks
- 1⅛ yards of cream-and-yellow print for outer border
- ½ yard of yellow print for inner border
- ½ yard of dark yellow print for binding
- 3¼ yards of fabric for backing (2 widths pieced horizontally)
- 57" x 75" piece of batting

Cutting

From the assorted yellow prints, cut:
- 12 squares, 10¼" x 10¼"; cut each square twice diagonally to yield 48 quarter-square triangles

From the cream print, cut:
- 12 squares, 10¼" x 10¼"; cut each square twice diagonally to yield 48 quarter-square triangles

From the yellow print, cut:
- 5 strips, 2½" x 42"

From the cream-and-yellow print, cut:
- 6 strips, 5½" x 42"

From the dark yellow print, cut:
- 6 strips, 2¼" x 42"

Making the Blocks

1. Sew a yellow triangle to a cream triangle as shown. Press toward the yellow triangle. Make 48 triangle units.

Make 48.

2. Sew two triangle units together. Press. Make 24 blocks.

Make 24.

Quilt-Top Assembly

1. Arrange the blocks into six rows of four blocks each. Sew the blocks into rows and press toward the yellow print in each row.

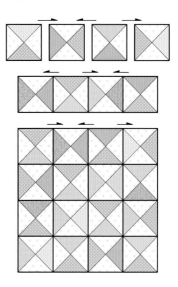

2. Sew the rows together and press the seams in either direction.

Adding the Borders

1. Sew the yellow 2½" x 42" strips together end to end and press. Refer to "Adding Borders" on page 9 to cut and sew the inner border.

2. Repeat step 1 using the cream-and-yellow strips to add the outer border.

Finishing the Quilt

Layer and baste your quilt, and quilt as desired. Referring to "Straight-Grain Binding" on page 12, prepare the dark yellow binding and sew it to the quilt.

Summertime Picnic Quilt

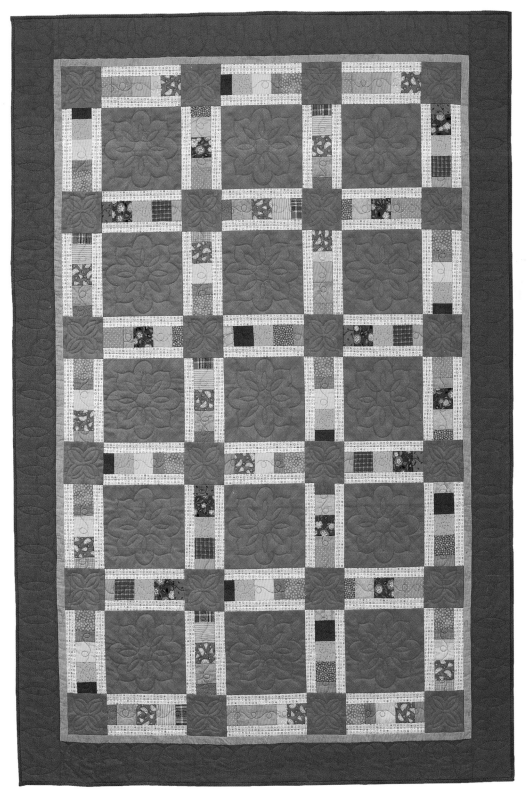

Designed and sewn by Julie Popa. Quilted by Paula Murray.

Make this quilt to spread out at those fun summer picnics. This project is quick and easy to sew together and would look great in any color scheme.

Finished Quilt: 50" x 74"

Materials

All yardages are based on 42"-wide fabric.

- 1½ yards of red print #1 for plain blocks
- 1 yard *total* of prints in assorted colors for pieced sashing
- 1 yard of white print for sashing frames
- ⅞ yard of red print #2 for outer border
- ⅓ yard of lime green print for inner border
- ⅝ yard of red print #3 for binding
- 3⅛ yards of backing fabric (2 widths pieced horizontally)
- 56" x 80" piece of batting

Cutting

From the prints in assorted colors, cut:
- 9 strips, 2½" x 42"; cut in half crosswise to yield 18 strips, 2½" x 21"
- 6 strips, 1½" x 42"; cut in half crosswise yield 12 strips, 1½" x 21"

From the white print, cut:
- 19 strips, 1½" x 42"; crosscut into 76 rectangles, 1½" x 8½"

From red print #1, cut:
- 4 strips, 8½" x 42"; crosscut into 15 squares, 8½" x 8½"
- 3 strips, 4½" x 42"; crosscut into 24 squares, 4½" x 4½"

From the lime green print, cut:
- 6 strips, 1¼" x 42"

From red print #2, cut:
- 6 strips, 4½" x 42"

From red print #3, cut:
- 7 strips, 2¼" x 42"

Making the Blocks

1. Sew together three assorted-color 2½" x 21" strips and two assorted-color 1½" x 21" strips in *random order* to make one strip set. Press all seams to one side. Make six strip sets.

Make 6.

2. From the strip sets, cut 38 segments, 2½" wide.

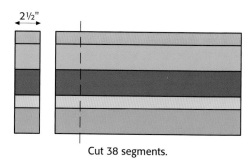

Cut 38 segments.

3. Sew a white rectangle to each long edge of a strip segment as shown. Press toward the white rectangles. Make 38 units.

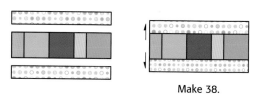

Make 38.

Quilt-Top Assembly

1. Refer to the quilt diagram on page 59 to arrange the 8½" squares of red #1, the 4½" squares of red #1, and the strip segments into block and sashing rows.

2. Sew the units into rows and press toward the red squares in both the block and sashing rows.

3. Sew the rows together and press toward the block rows.

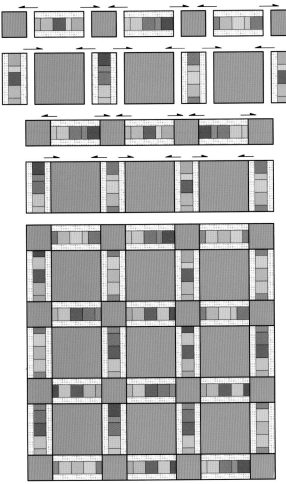

Adding the Borders

1. Sew the lime green strips together end to end and press. Refer to "Adding Borders" on page 9 to cut and sew the inner borders.

2. Repeat step 1 using the 4½" x 42" strips of red print #2 to add the outer border.

Finishing the Quilt

Layer and baste your quilt, and quilt as desired. Referring to "Straight-Grain Binding" on page 12, prepare the red print #3 binding and sew it to the quilt.

Cherries Wool Table Runner

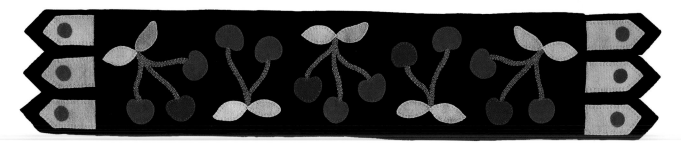

Designed by Julie Popa. Sewn by Julie Popa and Bette Popa.

Make this lighthearted project to brighten your table throughout the summer season. This project can also be stitched quickly for a gift.

Finished Project: 9" x 47½"

Materials

Cotton yardage is based on 42"-wide fabric. Wool yardages are based on 54"-wide fabric.

- ½ yard of black wool for background and large tongues
- ¼ yard of green wool for leaves and small tongues
- ¼ yard of brown wool for stems
- Assorted scraps of red wool for cherries and dots
- 1⅓ yards of black cotton fabric for backing
- Embroidery floss to match appliqués

Cutting

From the prepared black wool, cut:
- 1 rectangle, 10" x 37½"

From the lengthwise grain of the black cotton fabric, cut:
- 1 rectangle, 10" x 37½"

Appliqué

1. Refer to "Wool Appliqué by Hand" on page 6 for specific appliqué instructions. Refer to the cherry patterns on pages 61–62 and the tongue patterns on page 62 to cut the following from prepared wool:

   - 13 cherries from red wool
   - 6 dots from red wool
   - 2 and 1 reversed of stem A from brown wool
   - 1 and 1 reversed of stem B from brown wool
   - 10 leaves from green wool
   - 6 small tongues from green wool
   - 12 large tongues from black wool

2. Refer to the photo above to position the appliqué shapes on the black wool rectangle. Sew the shapes in place using a blanket stitch. Add accent stitching to the leaves. Use a ladder stitch to sew the vines.

3. Sew a red dot to a small green tongue using a buttonhole stitch. Make six small appliquéd tongues.

4. Sew a green tongue to a large black tongue using a buttonhole stitch. Make six large appliquéd tongues.

5. Sew one of the remaining black tongues to the back of each large appliquéd tongue, using a buttonhole stitch around all raw edges except the straight end (which will be hidden).

Make 6.

Making the Project

1. Fold under each edge of the appliquéd black rectangle ½" and press all around. Repeat with the black cotton rectangle.

2. Place the wool rectangle wrong sides together with the cotton rectangle. Pin in place.

3. Insert a tongue so that ½" of the straight end is tucked between the top and the backing.

Position three tongues at each end of the runner as shown and pin in place.

4. Using a blanket stitch, sew around the edges of the black wool rectangle.

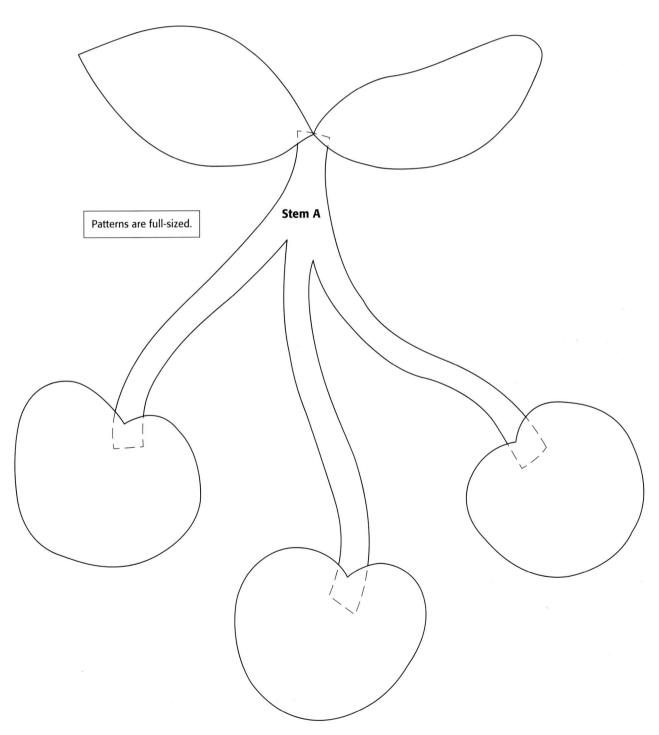

Patterns are full-sized.

Stem A

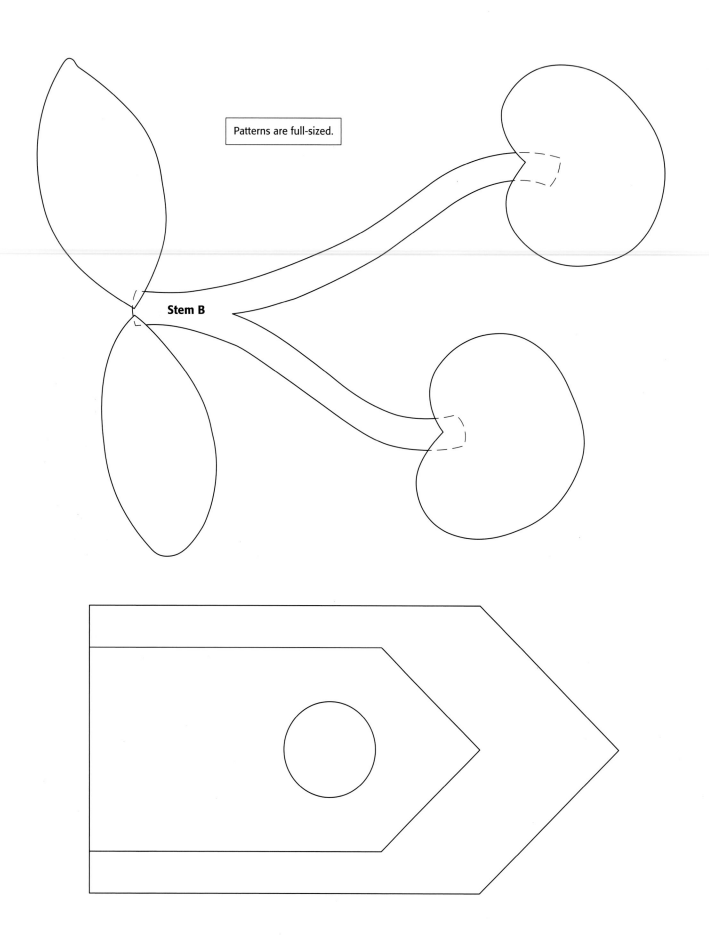

Patterns are full-sized.

Stem B

Fruit Salad Wall Hanging

Designed and sewn by Julie Popa. Quilted by Paula Murray.

What's a summer picnic without a little fruit salad? This quilt quickly became one of my favorites. It's fun to look at and easy to make.

Finished Quilt: 40" x 48"
Finished Block: 5⅝" x 5⅝"

Materials

Cotton yardages are based on 42"-wide fabric. Wool yardages are based on 54"-wide fabric.

- 1 yard of black print for outer border
- ½ yard *total* of assorted yellow prints for blocks
- ⅜ yard of red print for setting triangles
- ¼ yard *total* of assorted green prints for blocks
- ¼ yard *total* of assorted pink prints for blocks
- ¼ yard *total* of assorted orange prints for blocks
- ¼ yard of green dot print for inner border
- ⅛ yard of dark pink wool for vine
- 11" x 14" piece of yellow wool for pineapple
- 8" x 12" piece of light green wool for pineapple leaves
- 8" x 12" piece of medium green wool for pineapple leaves
- Assorted scraps of green, orange, and pink wool for dots
- ⅓ yard of green print for binding
- 2½ yards of fabric for backing (2 widths pieced horizontally)
- 46" x 54" piece of batting

Cutting

From the assorted green prints, cut:
- 12 squares, 3¾" x 3¾"; cut each square once diagonally to yield 24 half-square triangles

From the assorted yellow prints, cut:
- 6 squares, 4½" x 4½"
- 24 squares, 3¾" x 3¾"; cut each square once diagonally to yield 48 half-square triangles

From the assorted orange prints, cut:
- 24 squares, 2⅞" x 2⅞"; cut each square once diagonally to yield 48 half-square triangles

From the assorted pink prints, cut:
- 12 squares, 3⅜" x 3⅜"

From the red print, cut:
- 1 strip, 9¼" x 42"; crosscut into 3 squares, 9¼" x 9¼". Cut each square twice diagonally to yield 12 quarter-square triangles. (You'll use only 10.) Use the remainder of the strip to cut 2 squares, 4⅞" x 4⅞"; cut each square once diagonally to yield 4 half-square triangles.

From the green dot print, cut:
- 3 strips, 1¼" x 42"

From the black print, cut:
- 4 strips, 7½" x 42"

From the green print for binding, cut:
- 4 strips, 2¼" x 42"

Making the Blocks

1. Sew a green triangle to each side of a yellow square. Press toward the triangles. Make six blocks.

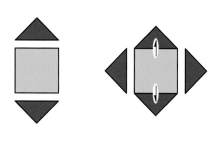

Make 6.

2. Sew an orange triangle to each side of a pink square. Press toward the triangles. Make 12 units.

3. Sew a yellow triangle to each side of a unit from step 2. Press toward the triangles. Make 12 blocks.

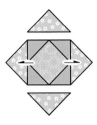

Make 12.

Quilt-Top Assembly

1. Referring to the quilt diagram below, arrange the blocks in diagonal rows. Add the red 9¼" triangles.

2. Sew the blocks and side triangles together into rows. Press toward the green blocks and red triangles.

3. Sew the rows together, adding the red 4⅞" corner triangles last. Press toward the triangles.

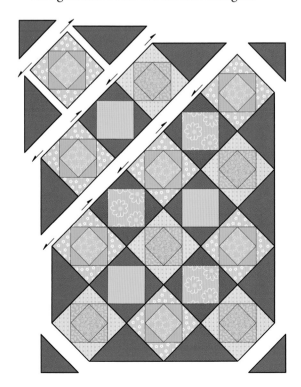

Adding the Borders

1. Sew the green dot strips together end to end and press. Refer to "Adding Borders" on page 9 to cut and sew the inner border.

2. Repeat step 1 using the black strips to add the outer border.

Appliqué

1. Refer to "Fusible Appliqué" on page 8 for instructions. Refer to the patterns on page 67 to cut the following from prepared wool:

    ◆ 1 pineapple from yellow wool (Note: Before you iron the traced fusible shape to the wool, cut out the inside of the pineapple ¼" from the drawn line. This will keep the wool soft, allowing the quilting lines to be easily added.)

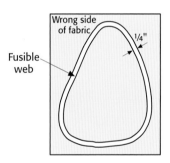

    ◆ 1 of leaf A from light green wool
    ◆ 1 *each* of leaves B–E from medium green wool
    ◆ 6 strips, ⅜" x 54", of pink wool (Note: Iron fusible web to the back of the wool before cutting strips.)

2. Refer to "Wool Appliqué by Hand" on page 6 to cut the following from prepared wool:

    ◆ 12 dots from assorted scraps

3. Refer to the photo on page 63 to position the pineapple and leaves in the lower-left corner of the quilt top. Pin in place.

4. Tuck one end of a pink ⅜"-wide strip under the pineapple and begin curving the strip around the border, using the photo as a guide. Pin in place. Butt ends of the strips together to form a continuous vine. Position the wool dots and glue them in place.

5. Fuse the pineapple, leaves, and vine in place. Secure them to the quilt using a machine blanket stitch.

6. Sew the wool dots by hand, following the illustration in "Embroidery Stitches" on page 6.

Finishing the Quilt

Layer and baste your quilt, and quilt as desired. Referring to "Straight-Grain Binding" on page 12, prepare the green print binding and sew it to the quilt.

QUILTING SUGGESTION

Paula quilted wavy lines in the pineapple and added X accents in the middle of some of the resulting grids. She then quilted designs resembling the pineapple leaves throughout the quilt.

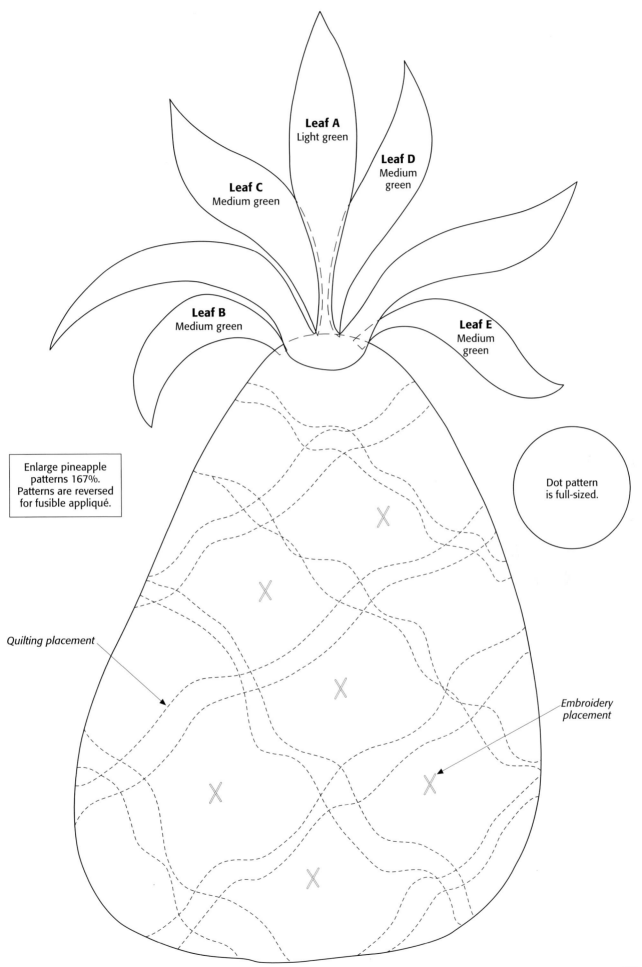

Leaf A
Light green

Leaf D
Medium green

Leaf C
Medium green

Leaf B
Medium green

Leaf E
Medium green

Enlarge pineapple patterns 167%. Patterns are reversed for fusible appliqué.

Dot pattern is full-sized.

Quilting placement

Embroidery placement

Star-Spangled Lap Quilt

Designed and sewn by Julie Popa. Quilted by Paula Murray.

Relive the days of 1776 with this nostalgic "star-spangled" quilt.

Finished Quilt: 52¼" x 65"
Finished Block: 9" x 9"

Materials

Cotton yardages are based on 42"-wide fabric. Wool yardage is based on 54"-wide fabric.

- 1⅜ yards *total* of assorted tan prints for blocks and border corner squares
- 1⅛ yards of red-and-cream floral for outer border
- 1⅛ yards of red print for blocks and middle border
- 1 yard of blue print for setting triangles
- 1 yard of navy blue print for blocks, inner border, and binding
- ⅞ yard of cream print for blocks
- ⅜ yard of yellow wool for stars
- 3¼ yards of fabric for backing (2 widths pieced horizontally)
- 58" x 71" piece of batting

Cutting

From the cream print, cut:
- 7 strips, 3½" x 42"; crosscut into 72 squares, 3½" x 3½"

From the assorted tan prints, cut:
- 72 rectangles, 3½" x 6½"; cut these in 18 sets of 4 matching rectangles per set
- 4 squares, 2" x 2"

From the red print, cut:
- 7 strips, 3½" x 42"; crosscut into 72 squares, 3½" x 3½"
- 5 strips, 2" x 42"

From the navy blue print, cut:
- 2 strips, 3½" x 42"; crosscut into 18 squares, 3½" x 3½"
- 5 strips, 1" x 42"

From the blue print, cut:
- 2 strips, 14" x 42"; crosscut into 3 squares, 14" x 14". Cut each square twice diagonally to yield 12 quarter-square triangles. (You'll use only 10.) Use the remainder of a strip to cut 2 squares, 7¼" x 7¼"; cut each square once diagonally to yield 4 half-square triangles.

From the red-and-cream floral, cut:
- 6 strips, 5½" x 42"

Making the Blocks

1. Draw a diagonal line on the wrong side of each cream square. Repeat for the red squares.

2. With right sides together, place a cream square on one end of a tan rectangle as shown. Sew on the drawn line. Trim the seam to ¼" and press toward the cream triangle. Make 72 units.

Make 72.

3. Repeat step 2 to sew a red square to the opposite end of a tan rectangle. Refer to the diagram to position the marked line of the red square correctly. Make 72 units.

Make 72.

4. This block uses a partial-seam technique. Begin by sewing a navy blue 3½" square to a unit from step 3 as shown, being sure to position the pieces together correctly. Stop 1" from the edge of the navy blue square and backstitch. Press toward the navy blue square. Make 18 units.

Seam ends here.

Make 18.

5. Continue to sew a unit from step 3 to each remaining side of a navy blue square, but this time use complete seams. Finally, finish the first seam. Press toward the navy blue square. Make 18 blocks.

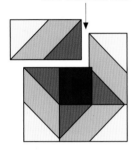

Sew this seam last.

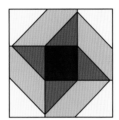

Make 18.

Appliqué

1. Refer to "Fusible Appliqué" on page 8 for specific appliqué instructions. Refer to the pattern below right to cut 18 stars from prepared yellow wool.

2. Fuse a star to the center of each block and use a machine blanket stitch to secure the shapes to the quilt.

Quilt-Top Assembly

1. Referring to the quilt diagram, arrange the blocks in diagonal rows. Add the blue 14" side setting triangles.

2. Sew the blocks and side triangles together into rows. Press the seams in the alternate direction from row to row.

3. Sew the rows together and press the seams in either direction. Add the blue 7¼" corner triangles last. Press toward the corner triangles.

Adding the Borders

1. Sew the navy blue 1" x 42" strips together end to end and press. Refer to "Adding Borders" on page 9 to cut and sew the inner border.

2. Repeat step 1 using the red print strips to add the middle border, noting the addition of the tan 2" corner squares.

3. Repeat step 1 using the red-and-cream floral strips to add the outer border.

4. Mark and cut scallops, if desired, referring to "Scalloped Borders" on page 10.

Finishing the Quilt

Layer and baste your quilt, and quilt as desired. Refer to "Bias Binding" on page 12 to cut a 30" square from the navy blue print. Prepare the navy blue binding and sew it to the quilt.

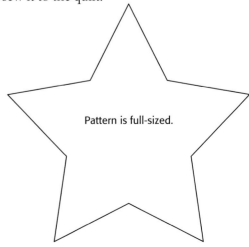

Pattern is full-sized.

America the Beautiful Table Topper

Designed and sewn by Julie Popa. Quilted by Paula Murray.

Make this red-white-and-blue quilt in time for summer celebrations, or use an entirely different color scheme to suit the décor of your choice.

Finished Quilt: 35" x 35"
Finished Block: 9" x 9"

Materials

Cotton yardages are based on 42"-wide fabric. Wool yardages are based on 54"-wide fabric.

- ⅞ yard of blue print for inner border
- ⅝ yard *total* of assorted red prints for blocks and outer border
- ½ yard *total* of assorted tan prints for blocks and outer border
- ⅜ yard of green wool for stems and leaves
- ¼ yard of white wool for stars
- Scraps of red, pink, and yellow wool for roses, rose centers, and star centers
- ⅓ yard of red print for binding
- 1¼ yards of fabric for backing
- 41" x 41" square of batting

Cutting

From the assorted tan prints, cut:
- 4 squares, 5⅜" x 5⅜"; cut each square once diagonally to yield 8 half-square triangles
- 1 square, 10¼" x 10¼"; cut twice diagonally to yield 4 quarter-square triangles
- 4 squares, 5" x 5"
- 4 rectangles, 5" x 9½"

From the assorted red prints, cut:
- 4 squares, 5⅜" x 5⅜"; cut each square once diagonally to yield 8 half-square triangles
- 1 square, 10¼" x 10¼"; cut each square twice diagonally to yield 4 quarter-square triangles
- 3 squares, 7⅝" x 7⅝"; cut each square twice diagonally to yield 12 quarter-square triangles

From the blue print, cut:
- 4 strips, 6½" x 42"

From the red print, cut:
- 4 strips, 2¼" x 42"

Making the Blocks

1. Sew a tan 5⅜" triangle to a red 5⅜" triangle as shown. Press toward the red triangle. Make eight units.

Make 8.

2. Sew two units from step 1 together as shown. Press toward the red triangle. Make four units.

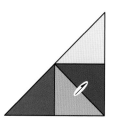

Make 4.

3. Sew a tan 10¼" triangle to a red 10¼" triangle as shown. Press toward the red triangle. Make four units.

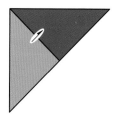

Make 4.

4. Sew a unit from step 2 to a unit from step 3. Press toward the two-triangle unit. Make four blocks.

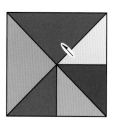

Make 4.

5. Sew two blocks together as shown and press the seam to one side. Repeat with the remaining two blocks, pressing the seam to the opposite side. Sew the rows together and press the seam in either direction.

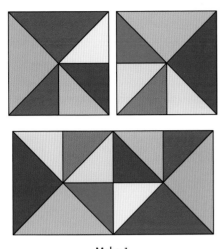

Make 1.

6. Sew red 7⅝" triangles to two adjacent sides of a tan square. Press toward the red triangles. Make four units.

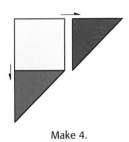

Make 4.

7. Sew a red 7⅝" triangle to one end of a tan rectangle. Press toward the red triangle. Make four units.

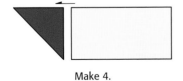

Make 4.

8. Sew a unit from step 6 to a unit from step 7 as shown. Press toward the tan rectangle. Make four units.

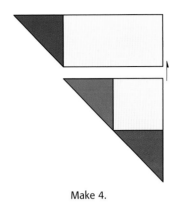

Make 4.

Quilt-Top Assembly

1. Refer to "Adding Borders" on page 9 to cut and sew the blue print inner border. Note that for this project you'll simply measure and cut one border strip per each edge of the quilt top, rather than sewing the strips together end to end.

2. Fold the quilt top in half in both directions and crease to mark the centers of the quilt sides. Fold the pieced triangle units in half and crease to mark the center of each one.

3. Match the center of one side of the quilt to the center of one pieced triangle and pin together. Sew the triangle to the quilt. Press toward the blue border. Repeat for the remaining sides of the quilt.

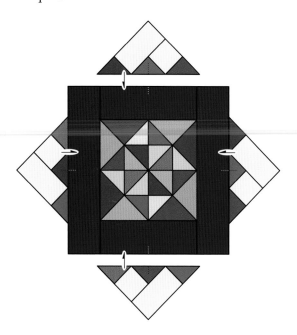

4. Trim the corners of the blue border even with the edges of the quilt top as shown.

Appliqué

1. Refer to "Fusible Appliqué" on page 8 for specific appliqué instructions. Refer to the patterns on page 75 to cut the following from prepared wool:

   - 4 stems with leaves from green wool
   - 4 stems with leaves *reversed* from green wool
   - 4 large stars from white wool
   - 8 small stars from white wool
   - 4 star centers from yellow wool
   - 8 roses from red wool
   - 8 rose centers from pink wool

2. Refer to the photo on page 71 to position the appliqué shapes on the blue border. Fuse the shapes in place and use a machine blanket stitch to secure the shapes to the quilt.

ORDER OF ASSEMBLY

It's easiest to fuse and stitch stems and leaves before you add the other shapes.

Finishing the Quilt

Layer and baste your quilt, and quilt as desired. Referring to "Straight-Grain Binding" on page 12, prepare the red print binding and sew it to the quilt.

Enlarge patterns 110%.
Patterns are reversed
for fusible appliqué.

Autumn Splendor Wall Hanging

Designed and sewn by Julie Popa. Quilted by Paula Murray.

When fall leaves begin to turn, it's time to bring the beauty of autumn into your home.

Finished Quilt: 66½" x 66½"
Finished Block: 12" x 12"

Materials

All yardages are based on 42"-wide fabric.

- 1⅓ yards of brown floral for outer border
- 1⅛ yards *total* of assorted red, orange, and purple prints for blocks
- 1 yard of cream print for blocks
- ⅞ yard of red-and-tan print for sashing
- ¾ yard of brown plaid for sashing squares and binding
- ⅝ yard of brown print for middle border
- ⅜ yard of black print for blocks
- ⅓ yard of red print for inner border
- 4 yards of backing fabric
- 72" x 72" square of batting

Cutting

If you'd like to make each block with the same fabrics throughout, the number of pieces to cut from matching fabrics for each block *is noted in parentheses.*

From the assorted red, orange, and purple prints, cut:
- 18 squares, 4⅞" x 4⅞"; cut once diagonally to yield 36 half-square triangles (2 squares per block)
- 36 rectangles, 2½" x 4½" (4 rectangles per block)
- 18 squares, 2⅞" x 2⅞"; cut once diagonally to yield 36 half-square triangles (2 squares per block)
- 9 squares, 4½" x 4½" (1 square per block)

From the black print, cut:
- 2 strips, 5¼" x 42"; crosscut into 9 squares, 5¼" x 5¼". Cut each square twice diagonally to yield 36 quarter-square triangles.

From the cream print, cut:
- 2 strips, 5¼" x 42"; crosscut into 9 squares, 5¼" x 5¼". Cut each square twice diagonally to yield 36 quarter-square triangles.
- 5 strips, 2½" x 42"; crosscut into 72 squares, 2½" x 2½"
- 2 strips, 2⅞" x 42"; crosscut into 18 squares, 2⅞" x 2⅞". Cut each square once diagonally to yield 36 half-square triangles.

From the red-and-tan print, cut:
- 8 strips, 3" x 42"; crosscut into 24 rectangles, 3" x 12½"

From the brown plaid, cut:
- 2 strips, 3" x 42"; crosscut into 16 squares, 3" x 3"
- 8 strips, 2¼" x 42"

From the red print, cut:
- 5 strips, 1¾" x 42"

From the brown print, cut:
- 6 strips, 2¾" x 42"

From the brown floral, cut:
- 6 strips, 7" x 42"

Making the Blocks

Although you may certainly choose to use the same fabrics in each block for a uniform look, I encourage you to vary the colors in each block.

1. Sew a black 5¼" triangle to a cream 5¼" triangle. Press toward the black triangle. Make 36 units.

Make 36.

2. Sew an assorted-color 4⅞" triangle to a unit from step 1. Press toward the large triangle. Make 36 middle units (9 matching sets of 4 units).

Make 36.

3. Draw a diagonal line on the wrong side of a cream 2½" square. Repeat to make 36.

4. With right sides together, place a marked cream square on one end of an assorted-color rectangle as shown. Sew on the drawn line and trim the seam to ¼". Press toward the cream triangle. Make 36 units (9 matching sets of 4 units).

Make 36.

5. Sew a cream 2⅞" triangle to an assorted-color 2⅞" triangle. Press toward the darker triangle. Make 36 units (9 matching sets of 4 units).

Make 36.

6. Sew one of the remaining cream 2½" squares to a unit made in step 5. Press toward the cream square. Make 36 units.

Make 36.

7. Sew a unit from step 4 to a unit from step 6 as shown. Press toward the assorted-color print. Make 36 corner units.

Make 36.

8. Arrange four middle units, four corner units, and one assorted-color 4½" square in horizontal rows as shown. Be sure that every unit is in the correct position before you begin piecing. Sew the units together into rows and press the seams in alternate directions. Sew the rows together and press in either direction. Make nine blocks.

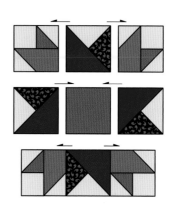

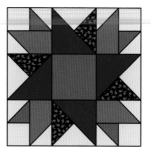

Make 9.

Quilt-Top Assembly

1. Referring to the photo on page 76, arrange the blocks, the red-and-tan sashing rectangles, and the brown plaid 3" squares. Sew together into three block rows and four sashing rows. Press all seams toward the sashing rectangles.

2. Sew the rows together. Press the seams in either direction.

Adding the Borders

1. Sew the red print 1¾" x 42" strips together end to end and press. Refer to "Adding Borders" on page 9 to cut and sew the inner border.

2. Repeat step 1 using the brown print 2¾" x 42" strips to add the middle border.

3. Repeat step 1 using the brown floral 7" x 42" strips to add the outer border.

Finishing the Quilt

Layer and baste your quilt, and quilt as desired. Referring to "Straight-Grain Binding" on page 12, prepare the brown plaid binding and sew it to the quilt.

Autumn Leaves Penny Rug

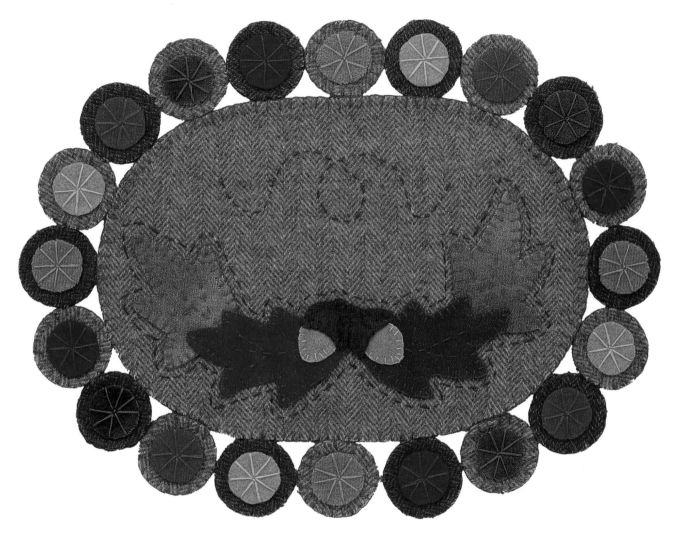

Designed and sewn by Julie Popa

Stitch this little project for the autumn season. It's a great take-along project that you can finish before the first leaves begin to fall.

Finished Project: 15½" x 11½"

Materials

All yardages are based on 54"-wide wool fabric.

- ⅜ yard of brown wool for top and pennies
- ⅛ yard of dark red wool for pennies
- Scraps of red, yellow, orange, rust, green, and dark brown wool for leaves, acorns, acorn tops, and small pennies
- Embroidery floss to match appliqués

Cutting *(Pattern is on page 81.)*

From the prepared brown wool, cut:
- 2 ovals

Appliqué

1. Refer to "Wool Appliqué by Hand" on page 6 for complete instructions. Refer to the penny and acorn patterns on page 81 and the leaf patterns on page 94 to cut the following from prepared wool:

    - 20 large pennies from brown wool
    - 20 large pennies from dark red wool
    - 1 leaf 4 from orange wool
    - 1 leaf 4 *reversed* from orange wool
    - 1 leaf 5 from red wool
    - 1 leaf 5 *reversed* from red wool
    - 2 acorns from yellow wool
    - 2 acorn tops from dark brown wool
    - 4 small pennies *each* from red, yellow, orange, rust, and green wool

2. Arrange the appliqué shapes on one of the brown ovals. Stitch the appliqués to the background using a hand blanket stitch.

Making the Project

1. Sew the appliquéd brown oval to the remaining brown oval using a hand blanket stitch around the edges.

Sew front to back.

2. Make pennies by sewing each small penny to a large penny with the stitch shown. Refer to "Embroidery Stitches" on page 6 for instructions.

3. Sew the remaining large pennies to the backs of the stitched pennies with a blanket stitch around the edges. Make 20 pennies.

4. Lay out the entire project on a flat surface with the pennies touching the center oval and each other as shown. Pin in place.

5. Using regular sewing thread (cotton or silk), take several stitches to connect the pennies to each other and to the center oval.

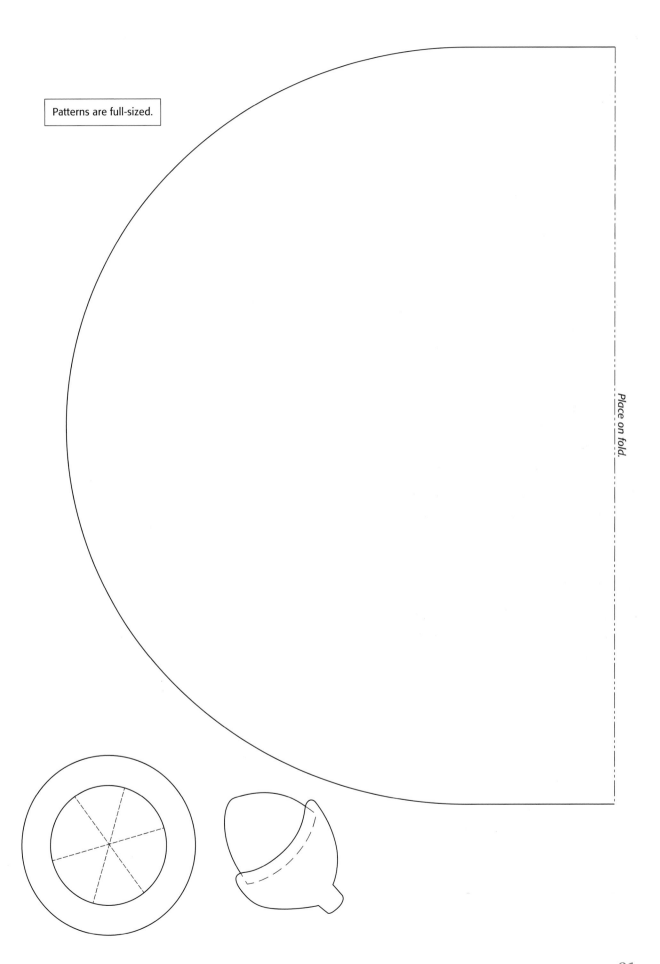

Patterns are full-sized.

Place on fold.

Fall Harvest Table Topper

Designed and sewn by Julie Popa. Quilted by Paula Murray.

This is a great table topper to help celebrate the Thanksgiving season and remind us of the important things in our lives.

Finished Quilt: 35" x 35"
Finished Block: 9" x 9"

Materials

Cotton yardages are based on 42"-wide fabric. Wool yardages are based on 54"-wide fabric.

- ½ yard of tan print #1 for blocks and pieced outer border
- ½ yard of tan print #2 for blocks and pieced outer border
- ⅜ yard of dark red wool for leaves
- ¼ yard of brown print for inner border
- ¼ yard of orange checked fabric for corner triangles
- ¼ yard of medium brown print for corner squares
- ¼ yard of dark gold print for pieced outer border
- ¼ yard of large-scale tan checked fabric for pieced outer border
- ¼ yard of yellow wool for leaves
- ⅛ yard of orange print for inner accent border
- 12" squares of 2 different tan fabrics for blocks
- Scraps of green, light brown, and dark brown wool for leaves, stems, and acorns, and squares
- ⅓ yard of dark brown print for binding
- 1⅓ yards of fabric for backing
- 40" x 40" square of batting
- Brown embroidery floss for lettering
- Assorted embroidery floss to match appliqués

Cutting

From *each* of tan print #1 and tan print #2, cut:
- 1 square, 10¼" x 10¼"; cut each square twice diagonally to yield 4 quarter-square triangles (8 total)
- 1 strip, 5" x 42"; crosscut into 2 rectangles, 5" x 17⅞" (4 total)

From *each* of the 12" tan squares, cut:
- 1 square, 10¼" x 10¼"; cut each square twice diagonally to yield 4 quarter-square triangles (8 total)

From the brown print, cut:
- 2 strips, 2½" x 42"; cut in half crosswise to yield 4 strips, 2½" x 21"

From the orange print, cut:
- 2 strips, 1¼" x 42"; cut in half crosswise to yield 4 strips, 1¼" x 21"

From the orange checked fabric, cut:
- 1 strip, 5½" x 42"; crosscut into 4 squares, 5½" x 5½". Cut each square once diagonally to yield 8 half-square triangles.

From the medium brown print, cut:
- 1 strip, 5⅛" x 42"; crosscut into 4 squares, 5⅛" x 5⅛"

From the dark gold print, cut:
- 1 strip, 5" x 42"; crosscut into 2 rectangles, 5" x 9¾", and 2 rectangles, 5" x 14¼"

From the large-scale tan checked fabric, cut:
- 1 strip, 5" x 42"; crosscut into 2 rectangles, 5" x 9¾", and 2 rectangles, 5" x 14¼"

From the dark brown print, cut:
- 4 strips, 2¼" x 42"

Making the Blocks

1. Sew two different tan 10¼" triangles together along the short sides as shown. Press the seam to one side. Repeat with two more triangles, making sure that you have used one triangle of each tan fabric. Sew these two units together to complete the block, and press. Repeat to make four blocks.

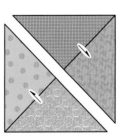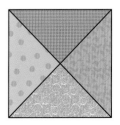

Make 4.

2. Referring to the photo on page 82 and the quilt diagram below, sew two blocks together and press the seam to one side. Repeat with the remaining two blocks, pressing to the opposite side. Sew these two rows together and press the seam in either direction.

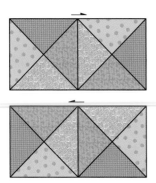

Quilt-Top Assembly

1. Sew a brown print 2½" x 21" strip to an orange 1¼" x 21" strip along the long edges. Press toward the orange strip. Make four strip sets.

Make 4.

2. Using a rotary ruler marked with a 45° angle, cut one end of a strip set from step 1 at a 45° angle as shown. Measure 19¼" from the point of the angle and cut the other end at a 45° angle in the opposite direction to create a trapezoid shape. Make four units.

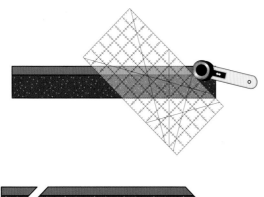

19¼"

Make 4.

3. Sew a unit from step 2 to each side of the center block unit. Press toward the strip units.

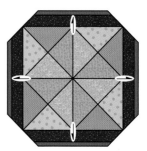

4. Sew orange checked 5½" triangles to two adjacent sides of a medium brown 5⅛" square. Press toward the triangles. Make four units.

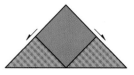

Make 4.

5. Sew a unit from step 4 to each side of the quilt center. Press toward the orange accent border.

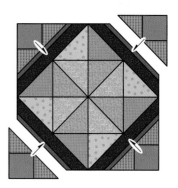

6. Cut the ends of a tan #1 rectangle at opposite 45° angles to create a trapezoid shape. Make two trapezoids. Repeat using the tan #2 rectangles to make a total of four trapezoids.

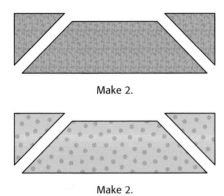

Make 2.

Make 2.

7. Place the dark gold 5" x 9¾" rectangles together, both with right sides up. Place the tan checked 5" x 9¾" rectangles together, both with right sides *down,* on top of the first two rectangles. You'll have four layers of fabric. Cut *one* end of the strips at a 45° angle as shown. Repeat with the 5" x 14¼" rectangles, placing the tan checked rectangles right sides up and the dark gold rectangles right sides *down.*

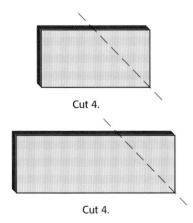

Cut 4.

Cut 4.

8. Sew a dark gold 5" x 9¾" shape from step 7 to one end of a tan #1 trapezoid from step 6. Sew a tan checked 5" x 9¾" shape to the opposite end of the trapezoid. Press away from the trapezoid. Make two short border units. Repeat, sewing the

dark gold and tan checked 5" x 14¼" shapes to the tan #2 trapezoids to make two big border units.

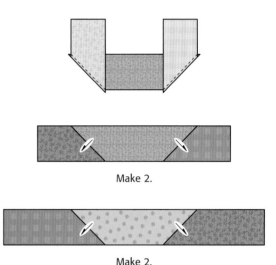

Make 2.

Make 2.

9. Fold the two short border units from step 8 in half and crease to mark the center. Refer to "Adding Borders" on page 9 to trim and sew these borders to the top and bottom of the quilt top, matching the centers of the border strips to the centers of the quilt edges. Press toward the borders. Add the long border units from step 8 to the sides of the quilt.

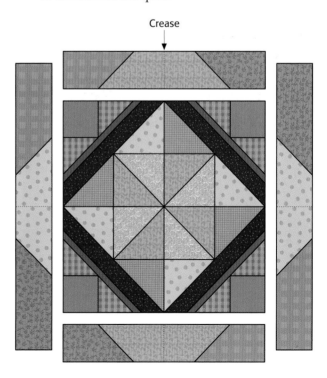

Crease

Appliqué

1. Refer to "Fusible Appliqué" on page 8 for specific appliqué instructions. Refer to the patterns on pages 86–87 to cut the following from prepared wool:

   - 4 of large oak leaf A from dark red wool
   - 4 of large oak leaf B from dark red wool
   - 16 small oak leaves from dark red wool
   - 16 small smooth leaves from yellow wool
   - 16 acorns from light brown wool
   - 16 acorn tops from dark brown wool
   - 4 squares from green wool
   - 16 stems from green wool

2. Refer to the photo on page 82 to position the appliqué shapes on the quilt top. Fuse the shapes in place and use a machine blanket stitch to secure the shapes to the quilt.

3. Refer to "Embroidery Stitches" on page 6 and the lettering patterns on page 87 to stitch the words on the quilt.

Finishing the Quilt

Layer and baste your quilt, and quilt as desired. Referring to "Straight-Grain Binding" on page 12, prepare the dark brown binding and sew it to the quilt.

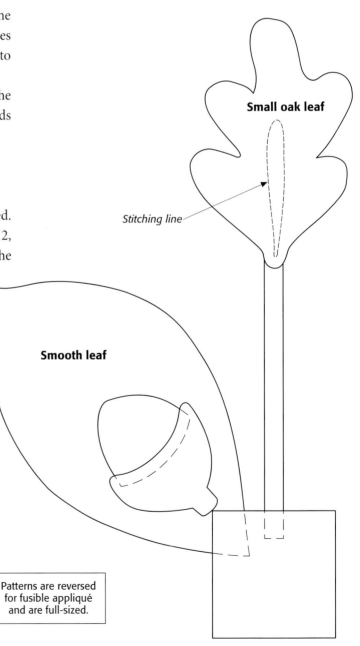

Small oak leaf

Stitching line

Smooth leaf

Patterns are reversed for fusible appliqué and are full-sized.

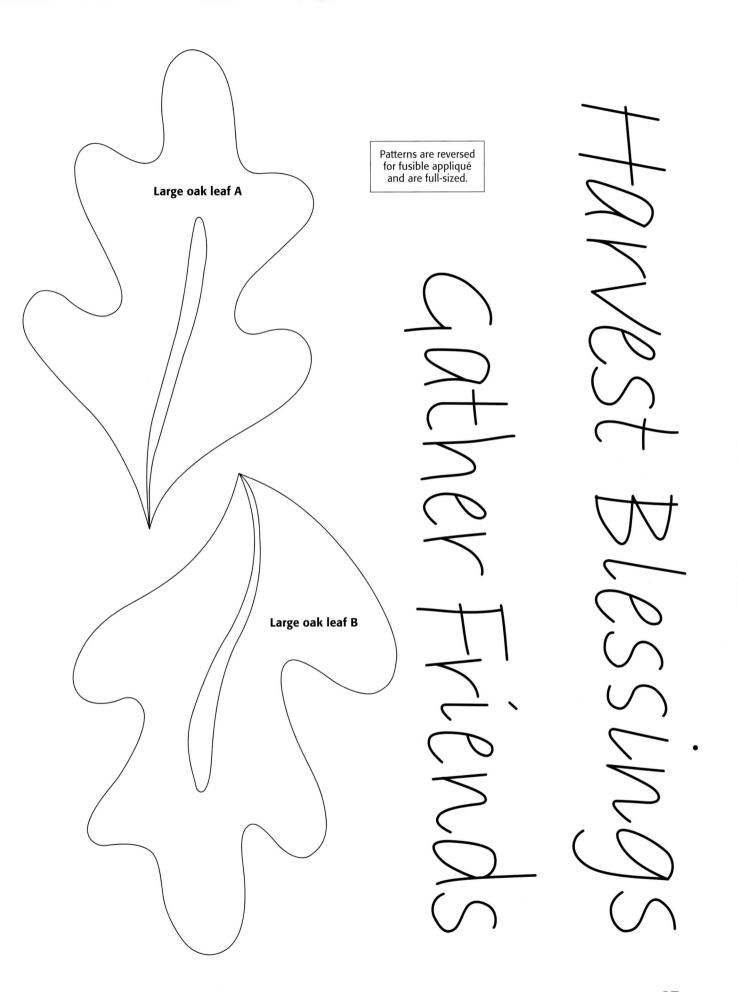

Large oak leaf A

Patterns are reversed
for fusible appliqué
and are full-sized.

Large oak leaf B

Harvest Blessings

gather Friends

Pumpkin Patch Lap Quilt

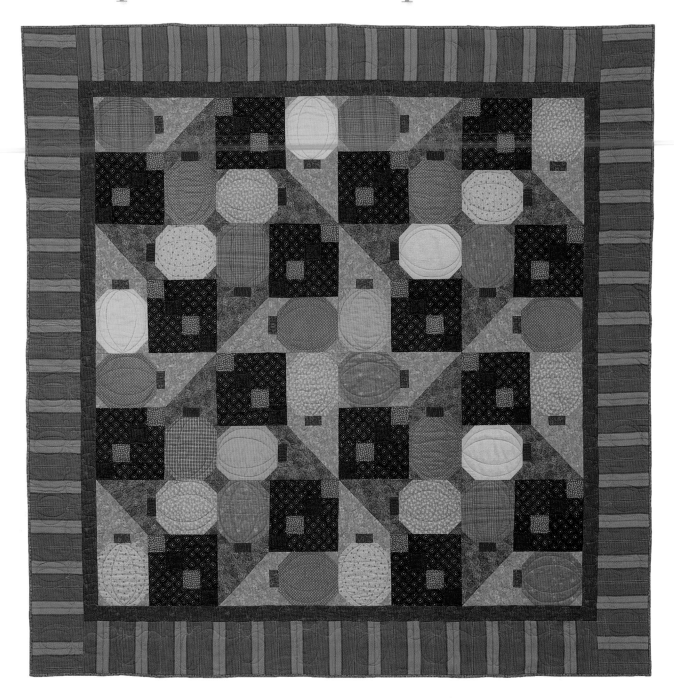

Designed and sewn by Julie Popa. Quilted by Paula Murray.

Finished Quilt: 80" x 80"
Finished Block: 14"

Materials

All yardages are based on 42"-wide fabric.

- 1⅝ yards of large-scale striped fabric for outer border
- 1 yard of black print for blocks
- ⅞ yard *total* of assorted dark orange prints for blocks
- ⅞ yard of dark green print for blocks
- ⅞ yard of light green print for blocks
- ⅞ yard *total* of assorted light orange prints for blocks
- ⅝ yard of bright purple print for inner border
- ¼ yard of brown print for stems
- ¼ yard of light purple print for blocks
- ¼ yard of blue print for blocks
- ⅔ yard of reddish orange print for binding
- 4⅞ yards of fabric for backing
- 86" x 86" square of batting

Cutting

From the dark green print, cut:
- 4 strips, 2" x 42"; crosscut into 64 squares, 2" x 2"
- 2 strips, 2½" x 42"
- 2 strips, 6⅞" x 42"; crosscut into 8 squares, 6⅞" x 6⅞". Cut each square once diagonally to yield 16 half-square triangles.

From the assorted dark orange prints, cut:
- 16 rectangles, 6½" x 7½"

From the assorted light orange prints, cut:
- 16 rectangles, 6½" x 7½"

From the light green print, cut:
- 4 strips, 2" x 42"; crosscut into 64 squares, 2" x 2"
- 2 strips, 2½" x 42"
- 2 strips, 6⅞" x 42"; crosscut into 8 squares, 6⅞" x 6⅞". Cut each square once diagonally to yield 16 half-square triangles.

From the brown print, cut:
- 2 strips, 2½" x 44"

From the black print, cut:
- 4 strips, 4½" x 42"; crosscut into 32 squares, 4½" x 4½"
- 4 strips, 2½" x 42"

From the light purple print, cut:
- 2 strips, 2½" x 42"

From the blue print, cut:
- 2 strips, 2½" x 42"

From the bright purple print, cut:
- 7 strips, 2¼" x 42"

From the large-scale striped fabric, cut:
- 8 strips, 6½" x 42"

From the reddish orange print, cut:
- 9 strips, 2¼" x 42"

Making the Blocks

1. Draw a diagonal line on the wrong side of a dark green 2" square. Make 64. Repeat using the light green 2" squares.

2. With right sides together, place a marked dark green square on a corner of a dark orange rectangle. Sew on the drawn line. Trim the seam to ¼" and press toward the green triangle. Repeat for the remaining corners of the rectangle. Make eight units. Repeat using the marked light green squares with the remaining dark orange rectangles. Make eight units.

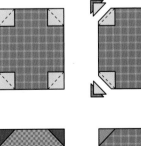

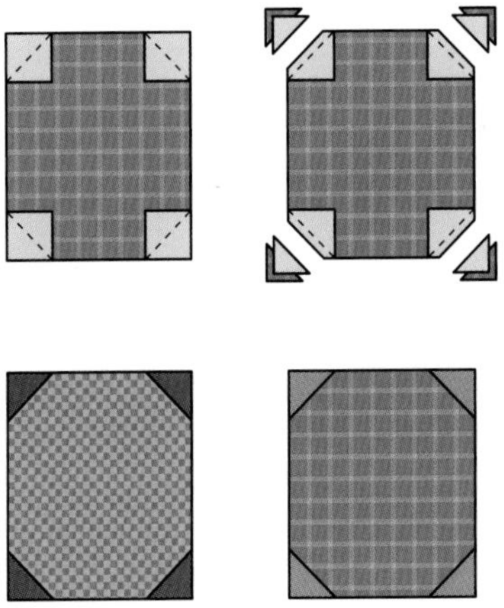

Make 8 with dark green corners.   Make 8 with light green corners.

3. Repeat step 2 using the light orange rectangles. Make eight units with dark green corners and eight with light green corners.

Make 8 with dark green corners.   Make 8 with light green corners.

4. Sew a dark green strip to each long edge of a brown strip. Press toward the brown strip. Cut 16 stem segments, 1½" wide. Repeat using the two light green strips and a brown strip.

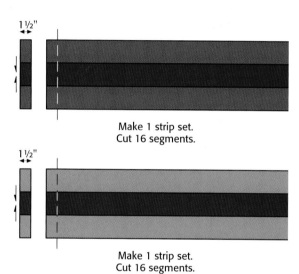

1½"

Make 1 strip set. Cut 16 segments.

1½"

Make 1 strip set. Cut 16 segments.

5. Sew a stem segment to a dark orange unit matching the green fabrics. Press toward the stem. Make eight pumpkin blocks with a dark green background and eight with a light green background.

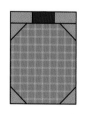 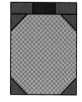

Make 8 of each.

6. Repeat step 5 using the remaining stem segments and the light orange units from step 3.

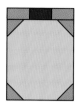

Make 8 of each.

7. Sew a dark green triangle to a light green triangle to form a half-square-triangle unit. Press toward the dark green triangle. Make 16 units.

Make 16.

8. Sew a black strip to a light purple strip to make strip set A. Press toward the black strip. Make two strip sets. Cut 32 segments, 2½" wide.

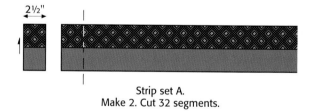

2½"

Strip set A. Make 2. Cut 32 segments.

9. Sew a black strip to a blue strip to make strip set B. Press toward the black strip. Make two strip sets. Cut 32 segments, 2½" wide.

2½"

Strip set B. Make 2. Cut 32 segments.

10. Sew together one segment from strip set A and one segment from strip set B to make a four-patch unit. Press the seam in either direction. Make 32 units.

Make 32.

11. Sew a four-patch unit to a black square as shown. Press toward the black square. Repeat. Sew the units together and press the seam in either direction. Make 16 chain blocks.

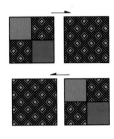

Make 16.

Quilt-Top Assembly

1. Sew a half-square-triangle unit from step 7 of "Making the Blocks" to a light orange pumpkin block with a dark green background as shown. Press toward the pumpkin block. Sew a light orange pumpkin block with a light green background to a chain block as shown. Note the orientation of the chain block. Press toward the pumpkin block. Join the sections and press the seam in either direction. Make eight blocks.

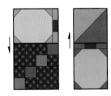

Make 8 using light orange pumpkin blocks.

2. Repeat step 1 using dark orange pumpkin blocks.

Make 8 using dark orange pumpkin blocks.

3. Arrange the blocks in four horizontal rows of four blocks each as shown below. Be careful to position the blocks correctly within the rows.

4. Sew the blocks into rows, pressing in the alternate direction from row to row. Sew the rows together and press the seams in either direction.

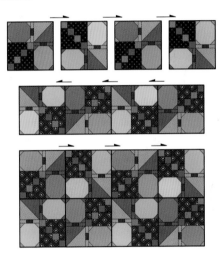

Adding the Borders

1. Sew the bright purple strips together end to end and press. Refer to "Adding Borders" on page 9 to cut and sew the inner border.

2. To add the outer border, repeat step 1 using the striped strips. Be careful to match the strips when joining the strips end to end.

Finishing the Quilt

Layer and baste your quilt, and quilt as desired. Referring to "Straight-Grain Binding" on page 12, prepare the reddish orange binding and sew it to the quilt.

Pumpkin Wool Table Runner

Designed and sewn by Julie Popa

Bring the sights and colors of fall into your home with this table runner featuring a trio of harvest-hued pumpkins.

Finished Project: 42" x 14"

Materials

Cotton yardages are based on 42"-wide fabric. Wool yardages are based on 54"-wide fabric.

- ¾ yard of black wool for background and large tongues
- ½ yard of black cotton fabric for backing
- ½ yard of orange plaid wool for large pumpkins
- ⅜ yard of light green wool for vines and leaf veins
- ¼ yard of light orange wool for small tongues
- ¼ yard of dark green wool for pumpkin leaves
- 10" x 12" rectangle of medium orange wool for small pumpkin
- Scraps of light brown and dark brown wool for stems and stem crowns
- Scraps of red, yellow, gold, and tan wool for autumn leaves
- Embroidery floss to match all appliqués

Cutting

From the prepared black wool, cut:
- 1 rectangle, 15" x 31"

From the black cotton fabric, cut:
- 1 rectangle, 15" x 31"

Appliqué

1. Refer to "Wool Appliqué by Hand" on page 6 for specific appliqué instructions. Refer to the patterns on pages 94–95 to cut the following from prepared wool:

   - 1 large pumpkin from orange plaid wool
   - 1 large pumpkin *reversed* from orange plaid wool
   - 1 small pumpkin from medium orange wool
   - 1 of vine A from light green wool
   - 1 of vine A *reversed* from light green wool
   - 1 each of vines B and C from light green wool
   - 1 each of leaves A and B from dark green wool

- 1 each of leaves A and B *reversed* from dark green wool
- 1 of leaf C from dark green wool
- 1 each of leaf veins A and B from light green wool
- 1 each of leaf veins A and B *reversed* from light green wool
- 1 of stem A from dark brown wool
- 1 of stem A *reversed* from dark brown wool
- 1 of stem B from dark brown wool
- 1 of stem crown A from light brown wool
- 1 of stem crown A *reversed* from light brown wool
- 1 of stem crown B from light brown wool
- 1 of leaf D from *both* red and gold wool
- 1 of leaf E from red wool
- 1 of leaf E *reversed* from *both* yellow and tan wool
- 16 large tongues from black wool
- 8 small tongues from light orange wool

2. Sew the appliqués to the black wool rectangle using a blanket stitch. Use the ladder stitch for the vines.

3. Sew a small light orange tongue to a large black tongue using a blanket stitch. Make eight large appliquéd tongues.

4. Sew one of the remaining black tongues to the back of each large appliquéd tongue, using a blanket stitch around all raw edges except the straight end (which will be hidden).

Make 8.

Making the Project

1. Fold each edge of the appliquéd black rectangle under ½" and press all around. Repeat with the black cotton rectangle.

2. Place the wool rectangle wrong sides together with the cotton rectangle. Pin in place.

3. Insert a tongue so that ½" of the straight end is tucked between the top and the backing. Position four tongues at each end of the runner as shown and pin in place.

4. Using a blanket stitch, sew around the edges of the black wool rectangle.

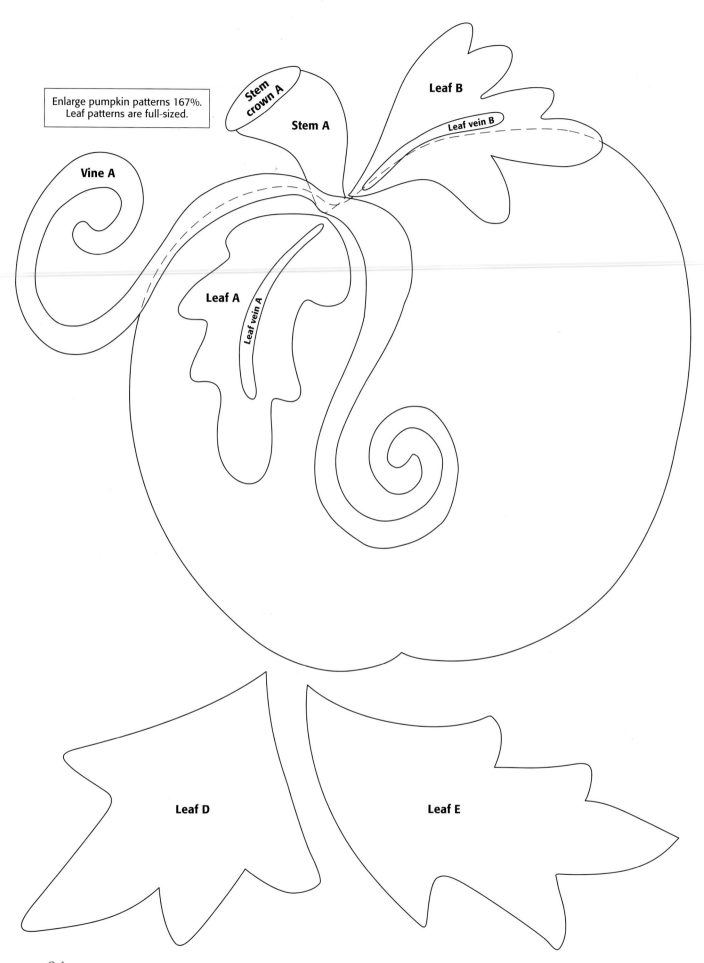

Enlarge pumpkin patterns 167%.
Leaf patterns are full-sized.

Stem crown A

Stem A

Leaf B

Leaf vein B

Vine A

Leaf A

Leaf vein A

Leaf D

Leaf E